D0331950

RECIPE
FOR
AMERICA

Ellen,
Thanks for all of your
support & all the work you
do.

RECIPE FOR AMERICA

Why Our Food System is Broken
and
What We Can Do to Fix It

JILL RICHARDSON

Brooklyn, New York

Copyright © 2009 by Jill Richardson
All rights reserved.

Printed in the United States of America.
This book is printed on recycled paper.
10 9 8 7 6 5 4 3 2 1

No part of this book may be used or reproduced in any manner without
written permission of the publisher. Please direct inquires to:

Ig Publishing
178 Clinton Avenue
Brooklyn, NY 11205
www.igpub.com

Library of Congress Cataloging-in-Publication Data

Richardson, Jill, 1980-
  Recipe for America : why our food system is broken and what we can
do to fix it / Jill Richardson.
    p. cm.
  Includes bibliographical references.
  ISBN-13: 978-0-9815040-3-2
  ISBN-10: 0-9815040-3-5
  1. Food supply--United States. 2. Sustainable agriculture--United
States. I. Title. II. Title: Why our food system is broken and what we
can do to fix it.
  HD9005.R525 2009
  363.80973--dc22
                                    2009020651

Dedicated to Eddie C and Jonny, and in loving memory of my brother Adam.

CONTENTS

INTRODUCTION

In March 2006, after reading several articles about the obesity epidemic in America, I decided to write a post about the issue on the popular political blog Daily Kos. To my shock, my post received over 600 comments! Obviously, I had hit on an issue that was on people's minds. While I realized that obesity was a result of poor diet, little exercise, and perhaps genetics, I wanted to learn why it had become so prevalent in this country over the past twenty years. After all, it wasn't like fast food chains like McDonalds, or soft drinks like Coca-Cola were new to the marketplace.

To try and find the answer to the obesity problem, I read one book after another, from *The Omnivore's Dilemma* by Michael Pollan to *Appetite for Profit* by Michele Simon to *Fat Land* by Greg Critser. The explanations these books offered for our national eating problem were numerous, which made me realize that there wasn't one single problem that contributed to the obesity epidemic, but several: marketers had gotten savvier; government policies now favored the production of cheap food; cash strapped schools had cut their gym programs and outsourced their lunch programs to fast food companies; and, as fewer families had stay-at-home parents, a higher percent of food was consumed outside the home.

I also discovered that the problem wasn't obesity alone. Pollan's book in particular made it clear that the same factors that had allowed our waistlines to expand also harmed the environment, rural communities, and agricultural animals. I began to realize that we had a *food system*, and that trying to solve the obesity problem without considering the effects that system had on the environment and the economy would be a waste of time. Yet, that's exactly what we do. While congressional hearings on obesity talk about limiting sugary beverages in school vending machines, they never discuss the fact that we devote only slightly less land to growing corn for high fructose corn syrup (1.2 percent of U.S. cropland in 2007) than we do to growing vegetables (1.5 percent) or fruits (1.6 percent).[1] As long as we're producing too much junk and not enough healthy food, making small changes in how that food reaches consumers won't change anything.

So what are the solutions, then? Some books, like *Diet for a Small Planet* by Frances Moore Lappe or *Animal, Vegetable, Miracle* by Barbara Kingsolver offer detailed steps that individuals can take, from changing their diets to growing their own food. Other books, like *Food Politics* by Marion Nestle or *The Omnivore's Dilemma*, advocate political change, but do not provide the details necessary to make that change a reality. Joel Salatin's *Everything I Want to Do is Illegal* offers the impression that everything would be better if the government would just leave farmers alone, but I don't subscribe to Salatin's Libertarian philosophy. And *Food Fight* by Dan Imhoff provides very specific information about the farm bill—but the farm bill is just one part of our overall food policy, and it only comes before Congress every five to seven years. Ultimately, I had collected an entire shelf of books on food, but none of them told me what kind of policies we needed to fix the problems in our food system. So, because that book didn't exist, I decided to write it myself.

Recipe for America is the book I wish I could have read three years ago, when I first began pondering America's problem with obesity. The first two chapters describe our current mainstream food system. Chapter one details my experiences as an eater, trying to achieve the not-as-straightforward-as-it-should-be goal of eating delicious, affordable, accessible, and healthful food. Chapter two tells how we have reached the point where healthy food is so difficult to obtain by providing a history of chemical agriculture and a description of the problems it causes.

Since this book is ultimately about solving the problems in our food system, chapter three describes that solution: sustainable agriculture. In that chapter, I talk about what goes on in the soil, and how it affects plants, animals, the environment, and ultimately, the food we eat. One of the biggest misconceptions about organic or sustainable agriculture is that it simply involves removing the chemical inputs from the soil, or replacing them with organic inputs, like worm castings instead of ammonia fertilizer. However, without a full understanding of how and why sustainable agriculture works, it is very difficult to defend it against those who advocate for chemicals or industrial agriculture.

Chapter four looks at the development of organic standards, which has allowed for the birth of Industrial Organics: certified organic foods sold by major corporations that are technically organic but not always sustainable. (As you will see, sustainable always means organic, but organic does not always mean sustainable.) Chapter five describes the various movements around the country that promote sustainable agriculture, while chapter six answers a question I hear asked all the time: if sustainable agriculture is so great, why isn't everyone doing it?

Unfortunately, supporters of sustainable food face numerous obstacles, some caused by nature, others that are man-made.

The remaining chapters therefore detail my plan for removing as many of these barriers as possible so that we can grow the sustainable food movement while simultaneously regulating industrial agriculture so that society no longer pays the price for its pollution, adverse health effects, abusive labor practices, and deceitful marketing. I've divided the plan into different categories: labeling, food safety, protecting children, human and animal rights, and the farm bill. Many of the recommendations I make reflect political battles that have been raging for, in some cases, decades. My effort here is not intended to imagine new policy ideas, but to organize and explain the ideas that are backed by experts and agreed upon (more or less) by the different groups within the sustainable food movement, and then explain how you can take action on these ideas. However, where I see gaps in existing ideas, I propose my own. Also, in some cases, while I could have gone a little bit further in what I am pushing for—for example, while I would like the U.S. government to ban the use of rbGH (an artificial growth hormone given to cows) in our milk, I call for allowing dairies to label their products as "rbGH-free" because I do not see the political will *at this time* for banning the hormone. Since there are literally infinite battles to wage, I think it is best to focus our limited resources on picking the fights that are winnable.

Speaking of fighting battles, in the three years I spent researching and writing this book, I made one very surprising discovery: our government is a whole lot more accessible than I would have ever imagined. It is easy to watch congressional hearings online or call a senator's office and speak with a member of his or her staff. You can also sign up online to receive emails when particular bills are moving through Congress, making it relatively simple to follow many different issues at once. And the USDA publishes an enormous array of data about every aspect of our food system, all available online. (In the appendices of this book, I share what I've learned about getting involved in our "food" democracy.) I hope that once you have finished *Recipe for America* and better understand the issues, you will join me in pushing our government to help us build the sustainable food system we desperately need for our health, our economy, and our environment.

1. FROM EATER TO ACTIVIST

Whenever I hear someone assert that healthy eating is a matter of individual choice, I reflect back to my life right after college. I had taken a low-paying job in Washington D.C., not far from the White House, and was living in a small room in Arlington, Virginia. Because of my circumstances—in particular, the lack of convenient transportation (I couldn't afford a car, and the nearest Metro stop was over a mile away)—within a few months of starting my job, my regular diet consisted of bagels, beer, Rocky Road ice cream, and the occasional banana. As a consequence of my poor eating habits, my body ached all the time, and my weight ballooned to 142 pounds, the most my 5 feet 3 inch frame had ever carried.

How could I have come to this point? How could an intelligent person like myself, who knew her way around a kitchen well enough to cook healthy dishes like chickpea curry, *choose* a diet of ice cream and beer? Surely it couldn't be lack of money; for the price of even the cheapest beer, I could still buy a few apples or perhaps some carrots, right? In fact, lack of money was not the reason for my poor diet. Instead, it was the lack of access to a good grocery store.

The condition of the grocery store near my apartment was

abysmal; it was stocked with the lowest quality produce imaginable, much of which was often rotting. And while the conventional produce was withered and lifeless, the "organics" were even worse. Despite the poor quality of the food, the prices were outrageously high—I can still recall my shock at seeing conventionally grown cherries selling for nine dollars a pound! On the few occasions where I was able to get halfway decent produce, it would usually rot quickly once I got it home. (I remember buying green beans one day at the store and finding them covered in mold the following evening.)

To try and remedy my "local" produce problem, I started taking the bus to more reputable grocery store chains like Trader Joes or Harris Teeter. Eventually, the extensive commute and long waiting times for the bus made those trips more and more infrequent. When I did get up the energy to take the bus, I quickly discovered that I could only buy as much as I could carry on a single trip, which meant, for example, that I couldn't purchase milk in the same shopping trip where I bought orange juice, as it was too heavy for me to carry both.

About once a month, a neighbor would drive me to Costco, Target, or some other store I couldn't access on foot, where I would restock my pantry. However, within a week or two of one of those trips, after eating all the fresh food, all that was left in my kitchen was a trove of candy bars, ice cream, frozen dinners, canned tuna, breakfast cereal, and "juice drinks." It got to the point where I wished that I didn't have to eat at all, as preparing a healthy, satisfying meal three times a day was just too difficult. As a result, beer and ice cream became dinner, and sometimes breakfast and lunch.

If someone had wanted to make the case that my atrocious eating habits were due to my own poor food choices, in a sense they would have been correct. On a societal scale, many groups make this very point, saying that poor people obviously have more than enough food to eat—since they're all so fat! Surely, I could have made daily trips on the bus to buy fresh vegetables, or located a farmers' market if I had really wanted to. In reality, though, the harder it is to find healthy food, the more likely it is that people will choose unhealthy alternatives. (When healthy eating required me to make frequent trips to the store by bus, I ate ice cream.) A study conducted by the University of California Los Angeles that tracked low-income mothers who received government vouchers for weekly fruit and vegetable purchases showed that their fruit and vegetable consumption went up, compared to a control group that was not provided with vouchers.[1]

Unfortunately, most low-income folks do not receive such incentives, and therefore few can afford to purchase healthy food. Adam Drewnowski, Director of the Center for Obesity Research at the University of Washington, believes that this is primarily a problem of economics, saying that "when you suggest that people buy rice, pasta, and beans you presuppose that they have resources for capital investment for future meals . . . a kitchen, pots, pans, utensils, gas, electricity, a refrigerator, a home with rent paid, the time to cook. Those healthy rice and beans can take hours . . . buying a doughnut for dinner does not involve any of those middle-class resources. You pay 55 cents for this meal only and there you are."[2]

In retrospect, I was lucky to even have had a local grocery store, rotting produce and all, when I lived in Arlington. In some parts of the country, people must either shop at convenience stores or else drive long distances to purchase their food. A friend of mine lives in one such "food desert"—a small town in the mountains, about fifty miles east of San Diego. He has to drive forty-five miles to the nearest food store, a Costco, or else purchase his food from the local gas station. Food deserts in urban areas have the opposite problem—plenty of places to eat, but usually only one option: fast food. A study entitled "Examining the Impact of Food Deserts on Public Health in Chicago" found that a resident of an urban food desert would have a difficult time following a doctor's dietary recommendations for healthy eating because of the lack of available food alternatives.[3] The study also found that, holding education and income constant, obesity increases as grocery store access decreases. "As communities become more out-of-balance in terms of food choices, residents are more likely to die prematurely and at greater rates from diabetes, cancer, and cardiovascular diseases, as well as suffer from obesity and hypertension."[4]

Airport Eating: From Bad to Worse

Eventually, I left Washington D.C. to take a job as a healthcare software analyst in Madison, Wisconsin. I thought my food troubles were over, as not only would I be making more money in my new job, but Madison was a far more affordable city to live in than D.C. I could even afford to buy my first car, making long bus rides to the grocery store a thing of the past.

However, while some of my food problems were now over, a new one sprung up to take their place. My new job required me to travel extensively, and I quickly learned that business travel and healthy eating do not mix well with one another. Complications come in two forms: the difficulty keeping perishable foods to eat at home when you are on the road so often, and, more importantly, the trouble locating healthy foods while traveling, particularly in the place where travelers tend to spend much of their time—the airport. Depending on the airport, the food situation I encountered while traveling ranged from somewhere between mediocre and horrible. San Diego International Airport, where I often traveled to and from, offered nothing beyond chains like Starbucks, Pizza Hut, Cinnabon, and McDonald's. Dane County Regional Airport in Madison was slightly better, offering bagels and micro-brewed beers. Detroit Metro Airport was even better, as my options there included Mexican, Mediterranean, even sushi. Minneapolis-St. Paul International Airport, where I spent countless layovers, was probably the best in terms of food choices, as it offerings included Asian stir-fry, Caribou Coffee, California Pizza Kitchen, T.G.I. Friday's, Chili's, as well as the French Meadow Café, whose menu was sprinkled with words usually not seen in an airport: organic, Fair Trade, and vegan. However, French Meadow was an exception, as most airports are overrun with processed and pre-packaged food. The traveling life would be much healthier if eating in airports—and on airplanes—could be avoided altogether, but when your flight only offers for-purchase brand name processed junk food, and your destination and departure airport offers only fast food chains, your options are quite limited. After a lot of frustration and a few food poisoning incidents, I learned to pack fresh fruit in my carry-on bag and avoid airplane and airport food altogether.

Once I reached my destination, I often faced another peril of the business traveler: the client lunch. These "catered" meals spanned the spectrum from the occasional salad to, in the worst cases, fried chicken, greasy sandwiches, and bean tacos as a "vegetarian alternative." (In fact, sometimes the vegetarian alternative meant picking the ham off my salad.) One time, at an office lunch in Wisconsin, I was served cheese as a side dish, and the only beverage offered was soda (or pop as we Midwesterners call it). While the office had coffee, I couldn't find anything other than non-dairy creamer to put in it. How could it be, I thought, that in America's Dairy State, I couldn't find something that came from a cow to put in my coffee?

The Spinach Incident

When I began traveling for work, I was not a vegetarian. At the time, I believed that I could give up specific types of meat as I saw the need to, without giving up meat altogether. Initially, I became picky about fish, as I didn't want to eat any fish high in mercury or PCBs, or any species that was endangered by overfishing. In order to do this, however, I often had to first quiz the wait staff at the restaurants I ate at. I won't forget the laughter of my coworkers as I stumped waiters by asking them whether the salmon on the menu was Alaskan or Atlantic. Later, when I gave up "factory farmed" beef, my decision provoked reactions ranging from raised eyebrows when I ordered nothing but a sweet potato at a Texas steakhouse to outright ridicule when I ordered a side of spinach at another restaurant and received an enormous bowl of steamed spinach that could have fed a family of four. Co-workers who witnessed the "spinach incident" were still laughing about it and recounting it to clients and new employees when I left the job two years later. Eventually, I decided to go vegetarian, if only to seem more polite at business dinners, as fussing over the origins of the meat on the menu and then ordering vegetables instead made me feel as if I was being rude to the clients and my fellow co-workers. Plus, as a vegetarian, I could give clients notice ahead of time to provide meat-free options for me when they chose a restaurant or catered a meal.

After about a year of business travel, I finally perfected an eating strategy that suited my lifestyle. When I was home on the weekends, I would visit my local farmers' market and buy anything that looked sturdy enough to withstand travel—so long as I could eat it raw or cook it in the microwave. In Wisconsin, this included foods like apples, pears, sugarsnap peas, bread, carrots, herbal tea, and corn on the cob. (One time, I even traveled with a cantaloupe.) Before the ban on bringing liquids ban aboard a plane took effect after 9/11, I would bring along peanut butter and honey. With this "stash" in my carry-on bag, I always had enough healthy food to satiate me until I could make a trip to a health food store in my destination city. I was also able to avoid the clients' catered meals by making a peanut butter sandwich or snacking on fresh fruit.

While I had proven that it was possible to live and work in the modern world while eating well, I also came to realize how much effort it required on my part to do so. How many people want to travel cross-country carrying backpacks full of carrots?

Outside of a small minority of dedicated "locavores" (people who are committed to eating locally grown food), most travelers choose their meals based on the options available on the road, whether it's the airport Pizza Hut or the catered lunch at a client's office.

From Eating to Activism

As a healthcare software analyst, part of my job involved obtaining lists of the most common reasons patients visited the doctor, as well as medical and surgical history items, medications, and procedures. Visiting clinics and hospitals across America asking for this information, I would hear doctors tell the same story over and over again: most patients came in with lifestyle-related chronic illnesses—including high blood pressure, high cholesterol, heart disease, type 2 diabetes, osteoarthritis, even erectile dysfunction—that could have been mitigated or prevented if they had improved their diets. When I asked doctors if their patients listened to their advice about changing their lifestyles and eating habits, they would typically answer "usually not."

Unfortunately, I was all too familiar with obesity and chronic illness even before I began working in healthcare. My father's side of the family has always struggled with obesity, and my brother Adam inherited the Richardson slow metabolism. While we always feared that Adam might one day have health problems if he didn't bring his weight under control, nobody would have guessed that he would be taken from us at the young age of twenty-three. We still don't know exactly what caused his death, but we suspect it was due to complications caused by his weight.

It was growing up with Adam that initially drove me to seek a healthier relationship with food. Since my parents were always concerned about his weight, food was a constant topic of conversation in our home. When he was in high school, Adam told me he was embarrassed because while his friends got in trouble for drugs and alcohol, he got in trouble when our mother found a case of Pepsi in his room. I felt there had to be a way to enjoy food without worrying that every bite might kill you, and after my negative experiences in Washington D.C. and as a business traveler, I was determined to find it.

By this point, I understood enough to "vote with my fork" by choosing to eat local and organic foods. However, the moment when my concern for America's food system extended beyond my own personal diet occurred on a business trip I took to Hawaii in January 2006. A large hospital on Oahu was installing my company's software, and they needed extra support to ensure that patient care was not compromised while their personnel learned how to use the new programs. I was assigned to the cardiac ICU, where I spent the next five days looking over the shoulders of doctors and nurses at confidential patient health information on the computer screen, all the while being surrounded by the patients themselves. To say the experience was eye-opening is an understatement. Many of the patients were tourists who had likely come to Hawaii for their dream vacation, only to end up in a hospital gown with tubes sticking out of every orifice of their body. One man was unconscious, breathing only with the assistance of a ventilator. Another was so gaunt he looked like an inmate from a Nazi concentration camp.

I didn't connect the condition of the people in the ICU to the food they ate until a nurse asked me to help her print out a "Heart Healthy Diet" handout she wanted to give a patient who was about to be discharged. While the diet encouraged the consumption of fruits and vegetables, the majority of the information was about how to avoid eating foods that most of us regularly enjoy. Trying to follow the diet would be nearly impossible at most chain restaurants (both sit down and fast food) unless the chef was willing to prepare you some bland steamed vegetables and a few ounces of chicken breast, with perhaps a side of brown rice. But then I suddenly realized that I already followed most of the diet. In fact, I loved healthy food so much that the highlight of my week had become my Saturday trip to the Dane County farmers' market, where I bought the fresh, organic, seasonal fruits and vegetables that made up most of my diet.

When I returned home from Hawaii, I started doing research about food-related issues, and came across four documents that would solidify my leap into activism. The first was the Center for Disease Control's statistics about obesity in America. Throughout my life, news headlines had shouted that obesity was an epidemic in this country. That certainly made sense to me, particularly because it had been such an issue within my own family. But I was unaware that, unlike other social ills such as poverty or hunger, obesity was a relatively new phenomenon. According to the CDC, less than 10 percent of the population of Illinois, the state where I grew up, had been obese in 1985; however, by 2007, that number had jumped to nearly 25 percent.[5] And Illinois was only 17th on the list—meaning there were 33 fatter states! What had happened? How could Americans have gained so much weight in just a few decades? Junk foods like McDonalds and Coca-Cola had existed for years, and human beings had surely craved sugar and fat since time immemorial, as those cravings are evolutionary adaptations that kept us from starving in times when food was scarce. Something must have changed during my lifetime to give rise to this epidemic of obesity.

With those thoughts on my mind, I started surfing the web. Eventually, I came across an article called "I'm Hatin' It: How the Feds Make Bad-for-You Food Cheaper than Healthful Fare" by Tom Philpott, a journalist and founder of Maverick Farms, a sustainable-agriculture farm located in the Blue Ridge Mountains. In the article, Philpott described how our government subsidizes programs that promote the growing of massive quantities of corn, and how that corn finds its way to our dinner tables in the form of cheap, unhealthy food. As he put it, "Our food system is shot through with corn." Philpott also pointed out the difficult choice that a low-income family often has to make at the grocery store when deciding whether to purchase inexpensive, but unhealthy food—in Philpott's example, a package of Ding Dongs (360 calories, 19 grams of fat, and full of high fructose corn syrup)—or healthier, pricey fare—a three ounce serving of wild salmon (185 calories with essential fatty acids, protein, and other nutrients). Obviously the salmon is more nutritious than the Ding Dongs, but if you've got barely enough cash to fill your belly, are you going to spend five times the money for one half the calories? And consider the ubiquity of those Ding Dongs in every convenience store in America, compared to the high end grocers that carry wild salmon—not to mention the difference in preparation requirements between the two foods. Philpott was onto something—food was political. The obesity epidemic was political.

This idea was reinforced by "Unhappy Meals," an article published in the January/February 2003 issue of *Mother Jones* that discussed how the National School Lunch Program, in addition to providing meals to children from low-income families, was also designed as a subsidy for agribusiness, and as a result often serves lunches that violate the USDA's own nutrition recommendations. The school officials interviewed in the article shared the frustration they faced from budgetary pressures, saying they often had no choice but to accept the free commodities (often cheese and meat, both high in saturated fat) that the government offered. I was outraged that our government would sacrifice our children's health in order to appease Washington lobbyists.

Though my initial focus had been on health and obesity, a third article broadened my interests to include food production. "Finger-Lickin' Bad: How Poultry Producers are Ravaging the Rural South" showed how corporations like Tyson take advantage of poultry growers and the rural communities they are located in by contracting with the growers to raise chicks provided by the company until they are large enough to be slaughtered. With few job opportunities for their citizens, many rural communities are willing to sign these risky contracts, even though over 70 percent of growers earn sub-poverty incomes and chicken companies are known to cancel growers' contracts (leaving them with massive debt) if they complain.[6]

Armed with these three articles and a healthy amount of outrage, I hastily wrote up a diary on the political blog Daily Kos, titled "Vegetables of Mass Destruction: Food, Poverty, and the Environment Edition." I promised to write a weekly series of posts about food and politics if there was interest from people in reading them. However, I could never have anticipated the reaction my diary would receive, or the path it would set me on over the next several years. "Vegetables of Mass Destruction" received nearly 300 comments, mostly from people who were excited to discuss food as a political issue. I read every single comment, and responded to as many I could, spending the entire week on a high from the outpouring of support.

For the next year, I posted a new diary every Sunday on Daily Kos while I spent the rest of the week searching for new topics, reading books about the intersection of food and politics, and visiting farms and farmers' markets. Obviously, I wasn't an expert at first, but my readers appreciated my enthusiasm and curiosity and cut me some slack when I made occasional mistakes. Because I was posting on a blog, I was able to receive immediate feedback for my work, and sometimes that feedback was negative. Whenever a blogger corrected a factual error I'd made, I would ask them to give me more information so that I could learn more about the topic.

Eventually, one blogger told me that his wife was a professor of nutrition, and he arranged for me to speak with her on the phone. She was the first person to tell me that there was actually a book called *Food Politics*, which I eagerly checked out from the library. I would have never guessed that I would one day meet the author of *Food Politics*, Marion Nestle, and that she'd be so lovely and gracious in person. But as it turns out, that's what the sustainable food and agriculture activist community is like—most people in the community, even the famous experts, are generous and willing to reach out to anyone who is interested in helping to reform our food system.

Today, more than three years after that first diary on Daily Kos, I know enough about our food system to call myself an expert. While I do not know as much about farming as a farmer does, nor can I recall the ins and outs of previous policy debates like those who have been in this fight for longer than I have, I now have a strong base of knowledge because I was able to stand on the shoulders of others in the sustainable food movement, all of whom took the time to show me their farms or recommended books they'd enjoyed or included me when they sent out press releases. Across this nation, there is an incredibly supportive community of food activists, and I've relied on them again and again whenever I needed to learn something new. If you are reading this book and are interested in becoming active on food issues, please feel free to reach out to me and I will gladly help you as others have helped me.

2. THE NOT-SO-GREEN REVOLUTION

I remember watching in amazement as a child the first time my mother made soup from scratch as, up until that moment, I had thought that only Campbell's knew how to make soup. Unfortunately, such ignorance of where our food comes from hasn't changed much since I was a kid. At a local food conference I attended in early 2008, a speaker shared a telling anecdote about how a group of children went to a farm one day to pick pumpkins, and one child asked why all the pumpkins were sitting in dirt.[1]

This lack of awareness of the origins of our food isn't confined to children, but has become prevalent among a majority of Americans today as packaged and processed food has come to dominate what we eat. As Ann Vileisis wrote in her book, *Kitchen Literacy,* during the course of the twentieth century "we went from knowing particular places and specific stories behind our foods' origins to instead knowing very little in an enormous and anonymous food system."[2] How our food reaches the grocery store shelves has become such a mystery to us that the Food Network made it the topic of a popular show, *Unwrapped.*

Despite my childhood ignorance of where soup came from, my family actually has a long farming history. I can still recall the stories my great aunt Kathy shared of the almonds, peanuts, blackberries, peaches, grapefruit, oranges, plums, apricots, mulberries, and olives that were grown on my great-great grandmother's farm, as well as the rabbits, geese, chickens, turkeys, pigs, and cows that were raised there. Far from being an anomaly, my great-great grandmother was typical of what was once a large swath of America as, at the turn of the twentieth century, nearly half of the population lived in rural areas, with nearly a third of the workforce involved in some aspect of farming.[3]

By the middle of the century, however, those numbers were changing dramatically as many American families—including my own—began to leave their agrarian roots in the past. Due to both the decline in rural living—today, only 10 percent of the population of the United States lives in what can be classified as rural areas—and the increase in the use of agricultural technologies like pesticides, irrigation projects, synthetic nitrogen fertilizer, and hybrid seeds, which I will talk about in detail later in the chapter—farming began to require far less manual labor and land than it had in the past. For example, in 1945, it took fourteen hours of labor to produce 100 bushels of corn on two acres of land. By 1987, however, it required only three hours of labor to produce that same amount of corn, using only an acre of land. By 2002, that same 100 bushels of corn could be produced on less than an acre of land.[4] Without need for his help on the family farm, my grandfather decided to pursue a non-farming career, ending my family's connection to the farming life. My family's story is similar to that of millions of other American families: in 1950, there were 5.4 million farms in America; by 1997, that number had dwindled to 1.9 million.[5] Today, fewer than 2 percent of Americans are engaging in farming.

As people left the rural life behind, the farms that remained, fueled first by the strong World War II economy and then by postwar international food relief efforts, expanded in size, with the ability to produce more crops than ever before. By 1958, one third the number of farmers was able to produce 55 percent more crops than they had twenty years earlier.[6] The reason for this increase in productivity is known as the "mechanical revolution," wherein farms adapted new technologies to their growing methods. These technologies included the widespread use of machinery such as tractors, the mechanization of activities that used to be done by hand such as hay bailing and the milking of cows, and, most importantly, the increasing use of pesticides.[7]

Between 1947 and 1960, the use of pesticides increased from 124 million pounds to 637 million pounds annually.[8] However, instead of improving the way we grow and eat food, the pesticide explosion helped transform what had been a sustainable food system into an unsustainable one, which, over the next half century, would move the inputs of farming from local communities into the control of multinational corporations.

The Birth of the American Chemical Industry

Prior to World War II, most of the food Americans ate was seasonal, local, and organic. This was by necessity, as before the technology was available to preserve, process, and transport food around the country (and eventually the world), there was little choice but to consume locally produced food. While railroads had long made it possible to import a small selection of non-local foods—mainly relatively nonperishable items such as grains—two mid-twentieth century developments opened up the entire country as a potential market for the agricultural industry: the vast highway system built during the Eisenhower administration in the 1950s, which made it possible to transport food more quickly and efficiently, and the post-World War II growth of the American chemical industry, which lead to the widespread use of pesticides and ammonia fertilizer on our crops.

In the years before World War I, only a handful of pesticides were commercially available, mainly pyrethrum, an organic pesticide made from chrysanthemums that is still in use today, and arsenicals.[9] Although available before 1800, pyrethrum was too expensive for widespread use, as the flowers used to make it had to be picked by hand.[10] An arsenic based pesticide called Paris green became popular in the United States during the 1860's, used primarily against the Colorado potato beetle. The next half century saw an increase in the use of Paris green (on apple orchards in addition to potato fields) and the development of lead arsenate as an insecticide used on trees to kill the gypsy moth.

World War I marked a dramatic turning point in the use and manufacture of chemicals. On April 22, 1915, during the bombardment of the French lines near the Belgian city of Ypres, a blue-white mist rose from the German trenches. This mist morphed into a yellow-green cloud, eventually blowing over to the French lines. The cloud was composed of chlorine gas, which the Germans had released from cylinders near their trenches. Modern chemical warfare had begun.[11]

By time the United States got involved in the war in 1917, chemical warfare had become far more advanced, with the introduction of phosgene, hydrogen cyanide, and mustard agents. In addition, livens projectors, artillery and mortars made delivery of the gas more effective, and deadly.[12] To coordinate the chemical-based warfare activities of the military, President Woodrow Wilson ordered the establishment of the Chemical Warfare Service in 1918.[13]

While Germany had dominated the global chemical market in the years prior to World War I, with the Germans now the enemy, the American chemical industry stepped up as a producer of explosives and war gasses. One company, Du Pont, fared so well during the war, supplying 40 percent of the propellant powders used by the allied forces, that North Dakota Senator Gerald Nye joked in 1935 that the next war would be fought "to make the world safe for Du Pontcracy" (playing on the World War I slogan "to make the world safe for democracy").[14]

Once the war ended, it was natural to assume that America's preoccupation with chemical warfare would end as well. For example, the 1918 executive order establishing the Chemical War-fare Service had also ordered the group's termination after six months. However, General Amos Fries, leader of the Chemical Warfare Service from 1920-1929, along with several key allies, including the American Chemical Society, were determined to make sure that research into chemical warfare continued—ideally under military control—and launched a public relations battle to highlight the peacetime uses of chemical weapons. "What we need now is good, sound publicity along lines showing the importance of Chemical Warfare," said Fries.[15] One of the chief arguments of Fries and his allies was that gas had important civilian uses, particularly as pesticides against insects.[16] Despite this claim, none of the pesticides developed and publicized during the interwar years proved successful when tested scientifically against agricultural pests. Nevertheless, portraying bugs as the enemy did succeed in muting the main moral argument against the use of gas—it's inhumanity.

The Second World War and DDT
In the late 1930s, a Swiss company called Geigy discovered that a chemical made from a combination of chlorine, hydrogen and carbon—known together as chlorinated hydrocarbons—was able to kill insects without supposedly being toxic to humans. In 1941, Geigy offered this chemical to its subsidiary in the United States, who initially declined to market it, as it did not believe that the chemical would compete well with an already available arsenic-based insecticide.[17] However, World War II would give this chemical, first known as Gesarol and later as dichlorodiphenyltrichlorethane, or DDT, a new lease on life. DDT would go on to achieve hero status by defeating malaria in the Pacific and typhus in Italy. Although other methods (like eliminating areas of standing water where mosquitoes bred) and other pesticides (including pyrethrum) also made significant inroads against insects and the diseases they carried during this time, it was DDT

that gained all the glory.[18]

With a need for DDT far beyond the production capacities of Geigy, the U.S. Army turned to other corporations to fill its wartime demand. Du Pont, which had been looking for a pesticide to mass market since the 1930's, seized the opportunity, though it refused to produce DDT unless it was assured a license to continue producing it after the war, which it received.[19] Other companies, including Merck and Monsanto, also received permission to produce DDT.

Once the war was over, the decision as to what to do with DDT was more or less left up to the companies that produced it. Despite several studies which showed increases in agricultural pests after spraying with DDT killed species that preyed on said pests, and other studies that reported alarming results when DDT was tested on animals—and which also feared the effects as humans ate fruit and vegetables contaminated with trace amounts of the pesticide over time—the War Production Board, the body that oversaw DDT production, nevertheless allowed "companies to sell DDT to anyone in any quantity."[20]

Silencing Spring

With World War II behind it, a grateful nation adopted chlorinate hydrocarbons such as DDT, as well as another family of pesticides known as organophosphates (parathion, malathion) for both agricultural and household use. The scientific community may have had reservations about DDT, but it was popularly hailed as "the War's greatest contribution to the future health of the world."[21]

Another legacy of the war, airplanes, were transformed from bombers into crop dusters, used to spray pesticides over large areas of land. Together, crop dusters and the new pesticides allowed for the spraying of crops for pennies on the dollar compared to the cost of the ground spraying of older chemicals.[22] By 1958, 200 different crops grown on an area that made up one-sixth of the cultivated land in the United States were being treated with over 900 million pounds of pesticides and fertilizers dropped by 5,000 crop dusting planes.[23]

From the start, however, there were warnings about the dangers of using pesticides. In 1945, biologist Orlando Park claimed that "if people killed enough insects with insecticides sprayed from airplanes, the loss of essential species would doom human life."[24] Unfortunately, the fears of scientists like Park were mostly ignored until 1962, when the publication of Rachel Carson's seminal *Silent Spring* marked a turning point in the story of pesticides.

In the book, Carson noted the deleterious effects visited upon communities that had been sprayed with pesticides in efforts to eradicate pests. For example, she wrote about how Clear Lake, California had sprayed its lake, a popular fishing spot plagued with gnats, with 1/70 part per million of DDD, a relative of DDT that was thought to be less toxic to fish.[25] Within five years, however, the gnats had returned, so the lake was sprayed again, with an even stronger application of DDD (1/50 part per million). That winter, western grebes on the lake began to die. In 1957, eight years after the first spraying, the lake was sprayed for a third time, and even more grebes died. Upon analysis of the deceased grebes, it was found that their fatty tissues contained 1600 parts per million DDD—a concentration 80,000 times greater than the maximum concentration that had ever been applied to the lake. "It was a house-that-Jack-build sequence, in which the large carnivores had eaten the smaller carnivores, that had eaten the herbivores, that had eaten the plankton, that had absorbed the poison from the water . . . No trace of DDD could be found in the water shortly after the last application of the chemical. But the poison had not really left the lake; it had merely gone into the fabric of the life the lake supports."[26] Eleven years after the initial application of DDD, the number of nesting pairs of grebes in the lake had dwindled from 1000 to 30; the number of young grebes observed had fallen to zero.

In addition to demonstrating the deadly effects of pesticides on animal life, one of the most important contributions *Silent Spring* made was in showing how these pesticides were also harmful to humans. That pesticides are toxic to us should come as no surprise; after all, our bodies are similar enough to those of insects that scientists have used insects to test the toxicity of chemicals intended to kill humans in war.[27] In *Silent Spring*, Carson documents case after case of people who were poisoned by chlorinated hydrocarbons and organophosphate: a scientist who ate a minute amount of parathion as an experiment, only to die before he could reach for the antidote at his side; two Florida children who repaired a swing with a discarded bag of parathion and died the same night; men who died or went into convulsions after spraying with dieldrin to kill malaria mosquitoes; and a man who accidentally spilled a 25 percent solution of chlordane on his skin and died forty minutes later.[28] The saddest stories are of children killed accidentally by their own well-meaning parents, like two Wisconsin children whose father sprayed his potato fields with parathion, or a baby whose parents sprayed their house with endrin to kill cockroaches.

Unlike many of Carson's examples, most of us are not involved in everyday situations in which we might experience acute pesticide poisoning. More likely, we consume or otherwise come into contact with tiny amounts of these chemicals in our food and in the environment—amounts so small they are measured in parts per million. While such amounts may seem insignificant, Carson makes two points that show you why they are not: first, pesticides and other chemicals accumulate as they move up the food chain; and second, our bodies are affected by chemicals even in such small amounts. For example, organophosphates act as neurotoxins, so while a small amount may not kill, it will still have an effect upon the nervous system. In *Silent Spring*, Carson offers the example of an alfalfa field sprayed with DDT. If a cow eats the alfalfa, the DDT may turn up in the cow's milk as 3 parts per million, but because DDT stores in fat, it may be as high as 65 parts per million in butter made with the milk.[29] Of course, the person who drinks that cow's milk will not drink it just once, but will probably drink the milk daily, and then store the DDT in his or her own fat, where it accumulates over time, and may be transmitted it to an infant via breast milk.

"Nature's In My Way"

By exposing DDT's harmful effects on the environment, *Silent Spring* brought about the end of the era of DDT in America. The Environmental Protection Agency banned most domestic uses of the pesticide in 1972, with several other chlorinated hydrocarbons following soon thereafter.[30] However, the lesson gleaned by pesticide manufacturers was not a rejection of their products, as they had won a lasting victory in the court of public opinion, as many Americans continue to this day to believe that pesticides are required to grow crops and that our best hope is finding chemicals that harm humans and the environment as little as possible while effectively killing pests.

Jim Goodman, an organic dairy farmer in Wisconsin, calls this method of agriculture "nature's in my way." With quick, easy techno-fixes like GMOs (genetically modified organisms), ammonia fertilizer, and pesticides, humans continue to improve short-term output even as they jeopardize the land's ability to produce food over the long term. This type of agriculture views nature as a machine instead of part of the web of life. In this paradigm, nature the machine can accept simple chemical inputs like pesticides and fertilizer and will always return an identical, natural output. However, nature always gets the last laugh, as following these methods erodes the soil and allows carbon to build up in the atmosphere. Furthermore, the inputs of agriculture, which used to be free as farmers saved seeds and used animal manure and compost to fertilize crops, now reside for the most part in the hands of major corporations.

And, despite Carson's dire warnings in 1962, some of the pesticides chronicled in *Silent Spring* are still in use today (such as malathion), as are newer pesticides that do not persist in the environment as long as DDT and therefore do not kill wildlife and humans so easily and obviously. For example, Monsanto touts that glyphosate, the main ingredient in its herbicide Roundup, breaks down quickly in the environment, preventing the type of bioaccumulation that killed the grebes in Clear Lake.[31] When farmers use Roundup, they often pair it with Roundup Ready genetically modified crops, also produced by Monsanto. While the Roundup Ready seeds can withstand the spraying of Roundup, no other plant form can survive in this kind of toxic environment.[32]

In addition, many pesticides are legal in specific quantities believed to minimize risk to humans and to the environment, some of which are sold to home gardeners, who can then use them in as high a concentration as they wish. According to Tyrone B. Hayes, Professor of Integrative Biology at the University of California, Berkeley, atrazine, the world's favorite weed killer, disrupts the sexual development of male frogs at levels of 0.1 ppb (parts per billion), but appears in U.S. groundwater in levels as high as 21 ppb. [33] While a number of European countries have banned atrazine, it is still legal in the United States. (The EPA is currently reviewing epidemiological studies examining whether atrazine causes cancer, and states on its website that it does not believe that atrazine affects amphibian gonadal development).[34]

It would require a near infinite amount of testing to determine whether the pesticides we are exposed to today through our food and in the environment harm us over the long term. It is one thing to test a single pesticide to determine whether or not it is harmful, but as Carson points out, sometimes a pesticide that is harmless on its own (such as malathion) may be deadly in much smaller doses when combined with another chemical. [35] Continued use of pesticides in our environment and on our food makes us each a candidate for a Darwin award that nobody should ever want to win.

Dead Zones and Factory Farms

Today, the effects of chemical fertilizers that are used throughout our nation's heartland manifest as a large (and growing) "dead zone" in the Gulf of Mexico. This effect is caused by excess nitrogen fertilizer that drains into the Mississippi River, ultimately spilling into the Gulf.[36] Tracked since its discovery in 1974, the dead zone (approximately the size of New Jersey) expands in flood years and shrinks in drought years, reflecting the amount of runoff carried by the Mississippi. Nitrogen fertilizers that reach the Gulf (as well as other pollutants, such as manure) feed algae, which eventually dies and sinks to the bottom of the ocean.[37] On the ocean's floor, oxygen-consuming bacteria break down the algae, removing the available oxygen from the water. Without oxygen (a condition known as hypoxia), marine life cannot survive. All organisms in the dead zone swim or scuttle away if they can, and die if they can't. Dead zones are not unique to the Gulf of Mexico; several others exist in U.S. waters, such as in the Chesapeake Bay—anywhere where pollutants support enough algae to create hypoxic conditions. Devoid of marine life, dead zones threaten the environment, as well as wreaking economic havoc on the fishing and tourism industries.

The dead zone effect is compounded by the excessive quantities of animal waste and pollution generated by Concentrated Animal Feeding Operations (CAFO). As defined by the Environmental Protection Agency, CAFOs (or AFOs, Animal Feeding Operations) are "agricultural operations where animals are kept and raised in confined situations. AFOs congregate animals, feed, manure and urine, dead animals, and production operations on a small land area. Feed is brought to the animals rather than the animals grazing or otherwise seeking feed in pastures, fields, or on rangeland." [38] A farm is considered a CAFO if its animals are confined for at least forty-five days during a twelve month period, and if there is no grass or vegetation in the confinement area during the normal growing season.[39]

While the number of farms in America shrank dramatically over the second half of the twentieth century, the number of acres in cultivation fell at a much smaller rate as the remaining farms consolidated. As these farms corporatized and industrialized, they started segregating crops and animals from one another. They also specialized more than ever before, either growing one or two commodity crops instead of a variety of crops that are rotated to manage soil fertility and pests, or raising only one breed of one animal. The popular monikers "industrialized" or "factory" farm fit these types of operations, as they view nature and farming as an extremely mechanistic process in which they can add identical chemical inputs and reap uniform output.

Whereas nature—and traditional diversified family farms— use animal waste to fertilize plant growth, and plant waste (such as crops that are unfit to be sold) to feed animals, factory farms raise either crops or animals in such concentrations that the normal systems of nature cannot function. For example, enormous fields of corn require immense fertilizer inputs, but in the factory farm model, there are no animals around to supply the fertilizer. At the same time, factory farms that raise animals can produce waste equal to the amount generated by an entire human city, and whereas this manure would normally be able to serve as fertilizer, factory farms generate it in quantities that exceed the land's ability to absorb its nutrients, as well as to attenuate any pathogens that are released into the soil.[40] A report by the Pew Commission on Industrial Farm Animal Production found that many factory farms "have not been sited in areas that are best able to cope with these enormous amounts of nutrients and pathogens. Many are found in vulnerable locations, such as flood plains or close to communities that utilize well water."[41] In addition, manure from factory farm animals usually contains antibiotics, hormones, pesticides, and heavy metals, which are destructive to the soil.[42] When the manure runs off into our waterways, it brings these contaminants with it.

Ultimately, the industrialized solutions that factory farms are forced to engage in because of their unnatural structure results in significant environmental damage that hurts all people (and animals), not just farmers and rural populations. As an example of this type of environmental damage, fisherman Rick Dove testified before the Senate in 2002 about how both his livelihood and his health had been impacted by pollution from hog CAFO operations.[43] After retiring from the Marines, Dove became a commercial fisherman near his home in North Carolina. His fishing career was successful for a few years, but in the early 1990s, Dove began to see scores of dead fish, many covered in bleeding, open sores, in the Neuse River, where he often fished. "There were so many dead fish that some had to be bulldozed into the ground," Dove testified. "Others were left to rot on the shore and river bottom. The stench produced by this kill was overwhelming and will never be forgotten." Eventually, the same sores that affected the fish began to appear on Dove's body.

In 1995, the number of dead fish spiked sharply, and volunteers cleaning up the river reported suffering from neurological and respiratory problems. Ultimately, it was discovered that an eight acre lagoon of hog manure had caused the fish kill by spilling 25 million gallons of manure into the river.[44] By this time, scientists had also uncovered the cause of the lesions: a one-cell organism called Pfiesteria piscicida that produces a neurotoxin poisonous to both fish and humans. The nutrients from the hog manure had allowed Pfiesteria to proliferate to the levels that killed the fish.

Since CAFOs often spray untreated urine and manure from lagoons onto nearby farm fields in quantities far too high for the fields to absorb them, the waste, with nowhere else to go, runs off into the surrounding waterways. According to the EPA (as of 2002), 60 percent of river miles, 50 percent of lake access, and 34 percent of estuary acres in the United States suffer from agricultural pollution, largely from CAFOs. Overall, 173,000 miles of US waterways are affected.[45] If hog CAFOs like the ones that damaged the ecosystem of the Neuse River were required to properly dispose of their waste, their costs would increase by $170 per hog, enough to make them far less competitive pricewise with family farms.[46] As Rick Dove pointed out, "There are myriad alternatives to the lagoon and sprayfield system, but the industrial hog barons refuse to adopt innovations that might cut profit margins."[47]

For example, a technique pioneered in Sweden involves raising hogs in a "hoophouse" with a dirt floor covered in a bedding material such as straw. During the hogs' lifetimes, their manure mixes with the straw and begins to compost. As manure builds up, farmers add more straw. An expert in this technique, Gary Onan, Associate Professor of Animal Science at the University of Wisconsin-River Falls, reports that hogs living in hoophouses are happier and healthier as they are able to engage in natural hog behaviors unlike in confinement operations.[48] Hogs in this environment require fewer antibiotics and suffer from lower mortality rates than hogs in CAFOs. When the hogs take their final trailer ride to the slaughterhouse, the three-foot high layer of manure and straw they leave behind is already half-composted. And as far as the financial bottom line is concerned, Onan noted that he made $14,000 from his hogs' manure, whereas a neighbor who kept hogs in confinement spent $10,000 to drain his lagoon and spray the liquefied manure onto a field. Unfortunately, pollution problems and the refusal to adopt alternative production methods are not unique to the hog industry, but exist across the board for all animals kept in CAFOs.

CAFOs also serve as breeding grounds for many of the food safety problems we encounter today, such as E. coli O157:H7, which can cause severe abdominal pain, bloody diarrhea, kidney failure, and even death. When cows eat mostly grass and hay, the E. coli in their digestive tracts cannot survive in the acid of a human stomach.[49] However, factory farmed animals do not eat grass or hay; they eat grain. In 1998, researchers at Cornell University concluded that cows digest grain poorly, allowing some to reach their colons.[50] In the colon, the grain ferments, providing an environment where acid-resistant E. coli can evolve. The researchers identified a simple, inexpensive solution to this problem: by switching cows' diets to grass or hay a few days before slaughter, most acid-resistant E. coli are eliminated. The researchers stated that this change would not impact the cows' carcass size or meat quality, yet more than ten years after the publication of these findings, cows in feedlots still eat grain until the day they die.

Detrimental Effects on Communities and Workers
While factory farms can be family-owned—just as small family farms can incorporate as a form of legal organization—for the most part family farms are smaller in size and utilize less hired help as a proportion of labor. In a family farm, the same group of people own, manage, and operate the farm. By contrast, in factory farms, the division of labor is segregated, as one group owns the farm, another manages its operations, and a third does the actual work. This organizational structure often traumatizes the communities where the factory farm is located, causing a host of harmful consequences, including the creation of low wage jobs that change the social class composition of the area. With the increase of income inequality, communities often see increases in crime, teen pregnancy and high school dropout rates, family instability, and other kinds of social disruption. As the tax base erodes in these areas, the schools, community services and infrastructure receive less funding; government spending, instead of going to residents of the community, is often disproportionately given to the corporation that owns the industrialized farm.

A famous example of this was reflected in a study centered

on two California towns, Arvin and Dinuba. In the early 1940s, an anthropologist named Walter Goldschmidt compared Arvin, with its many large, absentee-owned, non-family operated farms, to Dinuba, where most farms were locally owned and family operated. Goldschmidt found a smaller middle class, greater poverty, lower family incomes, and poorer quality schools and public services in Arvin. Dinuba, on the other hand, had "a larger middle class, better socioeconomic conditions, high community stability and civic participation."[51] A second study of the two towns conducted by the state of California almost forty years later showed the same results, with an increase in the disparity of the towns as compared with the first study.[52]

Most problematic, however, are the effects of factory farms on the people who are employed by them. While the working conditions of meatpacking plants are well documented in books like *Fast Food Nation* and *Diet for a Dead Planet,* I heard one such story firsthand from David Ward, who shared with me his experiences during the brief time he was employed as a meatpacker by Tyson.[53] Ward had been living in Chicago, finding work through a temporary agency, when he met a recruiter for Tyson. "They sell you a nice dream," he told me. Ward got a job working with ham—cutting it, removing the bone, packaging it up, and weighing it. A slow line required workers to handle one ham every 15 seconds; a fast line one every 11 seconds. "By the time you touch a ham, you need to let it go," Ward said. With such a fast pace, most workers sported injuries like neck pain and tendonitis from the repetitive motions they had to perform while on the job. Ward suffered from tendonitis in his right hand for several weeks, during which time he was unable to make a fist. In addition, he had numerous run-ins with plant management over unsafe conditions, which, according to Ward, eventually caused him to fall and break his ankle. When I spoke to Ward, he had hired to lawyer to try and force Tyson to pay worker's compensation.

In one respect, Ward is lucky, as he is an American citizen.

Often, factory farms hire immigrants (legal and otherwise) who are desperate for jobs, particularly ones that do not require them to speak English.[54] In the event that they are either injured on the job or treated unfairly, these workers have little recourse to legal action or worker's compensation because of their poor language skills, and because they may fear deportation if they speak to government officials.

Ironically, the owners of CAFOs are sometimes little better off than their workers, especially if they engage in contract production. In this type of arrangement, integrators (usually large companies such as Tyson) provide animals, feed, medicine, and transportation to growers (individual CAFO operations), who in turn have to deal with the rest of the process, including the costs associated with construction, maintenance, labor, and manure disposal. The integrators reimburse the growers based on measures like weight gain of the animals.[55] In contract production, the integrators hold all the cards. If a grower does not meet the integrator's demands, the integrator can cancel out the contract. On the other hand, if a grower takes issue with an integrator, until the passage of the 2008 farm bill, the contract often stipulated "mandatory arbitration," forcing the grower to take the matter to an arbitrator instead of going to court. "Arbitration is prohibitively expensive for producers, and limits their legal rights," writes journalist Tom Philpott.[56] Since only a handful of companies control each livestock industry, no competitor exists to provide growers with fair contracts.

Another livestock industry practice designed to manipulate markets in the favor of large companies is known as captive supply, where companies avoid buying animals on the open market by either owning or controlling livestock through contracts. When prices fall, the companies buy livestock from producers; when prices rise, they use their captive supply instead. This leaves individual producers with a dilemma: sell for a low price or don't sell at all. Taken together, contract production and captive supple provide insight into the inequality that results when industrialized food operations move into town.

The Human Cost of Industrial Agriculture

Even without going into the specifics, the effect of an increasingly industrialized food system on human health is easy to see. Between 1974 and 2004, the obesity rate in the United States more than doubled for children of all ages—and more than tripled for children between the ages of 6 and 11.[57] For adult men, the obesity rate during that same period increased from 12.8 percent to 30.2 percent; for adult women, it went from 16.8 percent to 34 percent.[58] At the same time, Americans went from spending 7 percent of GDP on health care in 1970 to 15.3 percent in 2004.[59]

Angie Tagtow, an environmental nutrition consultant, explains the link between the changes in our food system and the diminishing quality of our nutritional health by pointing out that without healthy soil, we cannot grow healthy food.[60] However, under our current industrial agricultural system, we have isolated the three nutrients that plants require for healthy growth—nitrogen, potassium, and phosphorus—and pour them onto our crops in greater than necessary quantities. While this makes the crops grow, studies show that the nutrient content of today's fruits and vegetables has declined compared to the fruits and vegetables of yesteryear. The apple of today may look like the apple of fifty years ago, but it contains only one third as much iron.[61]

We find a similar problem with animal products. How can a factory farmed animal's milk or meat possibly be the same as an animal raised on pasture and fed a healthier, more natural diet? (Michael Pollan encourages people to pay attention not only to what they eat, but to what what they eat eats.) In fact, studies show that allowing a cow to graze on pasture can increase the content of CLA, an anti-carcinogen, in dairy products.[62] Additionally, a study by Utah State University found that the meat

2. THE NOT-SO-GREEN REVOLUTION

from pasture-fed cattle contained 466 percent more CLA and 300 percent more Vitamin E as cattle fed the "typical high-grain feedlot diet."[63]

Overall, while our food may look like the same on the outside as what our great-grandparents ate, inside it is completely different. For example, a recent report exposed the antibiotics that are found in vegetables. While farmers have used manure from livestock to fertilize crops since the drawn of civilization, until relatively recently, they did not keep livestock in unhealthy factory farm conditions where they are administered antibiotics to promote growth and prevent infection. Almost 70 percent of all antibiotics produced in the United States today are fed to livestock—and about 90 percent of the antibiotics fed to animals come out the animals' other ends as urine or manure.[64] When we fertilize crops with antibiotic-laced manure, our vegetables absorb the antibiotics as they grow. And while these antibiotics may not directly harm our bodies, they do result in decreasing the effectiveness of human medicine by creating antibiotic-resistant bacteria.

The most famous superbug of this type is methicillin-resistant Staphylococcus aureus, or MRSA, a disease that afflicted 94,000 people, and killed 18,000 of them, in the United States in 2005.[65] University of Iowa researchers recently published a study showing an identical strain of MRSA that was found in 49 percent of hogs and 45 percent of humans caring for them on hog farms in the Midwest. The research indicates that MRSA can be shared across species, and the publication of the study opened a Pandora's box of questions about the safety of our meat supply—one that nobody has yet studied.[66]

In the end, the numerous problems in our food system—pollution, human rights abuses, poor food safety, the breakdown of rural communities, and the decline in our health—are hardly random. Instead, they stem from a common thread of industrialization, which occurred primarily over the second half of the twentieth century. No doubt my great-great-grandmother would be bewildered if she toured a modern grocery store or read an ingredient label listing unpronounceable words as components of our so-called "food." Her shock would multiply if she visited a CAFO and witnessed our society disposing of chicken litter and rendered slaughterhouse leftovers such as blood and feathers by repurposing them as animal feed.[67]

3. SUSTAINABLE AGRICULTURE

As we saw in the previous chapter, the face of agriculture has changed dramatically since the days when my great-great-grandmother operated her farm in the first half of the twentieth century. Without modern equipment and chemicals, working the land back then was relatively labor-intensive, with farmers using time honored growing techniques that had been in use for centuries. The common elements these techniques shared was that they were "sustainable," meaning they were designed to produce food that was healthy for the people that grew and ate it, as well as the land and animals, without compromising the wellbeing of future generations.

Of course, back in my great-great-grandmother's day, farms had no choice but to be sustainable. However, as unsustainable practices have taken over our agricultural system, a movement has emerged among both farmers and consumers that longs to create an agricultural model that is "resource-conserving, socially supportive, commercially competitive, and environmentally sound."[1] This movement is known as "sustainable agriculture."

According to the USDA, "sustainable agriculture" refers to an "integrated system of plant and animal production practices having a site-specific application that will, over the long term:

- satisfy human food and fiber needs
- enhance environmental quality and the natural resource base upon which the agricultural economy depends
- make the most efficient use of nonrenewable resources and on-farm resources and integrate, where appropriate, natural biological cycles and controls
- sustain the economic viability of farm operations
- enhance the quality of life for farmers and society as a whole."[2]

The sustainable agriculture movement asks several basic questions: can we continue to use pesticides, ammonia fertilizer, GMOs, and other artificial technologies to produce our food without hindering the ability of future generations to produce food? Can we continue to raise animals in factory farms and run our entire food system on corn and soy without harming our health? The answer has become clear: no, we cannot.

Imagine a large farm in Iowa that grows corn. Nothing but corn for miles and miles. Without a natural way to restore nutrients to the soil, the farmer must pour on fertilizer to make the corn grow. He must also use pesticides like atrazine. Some of the fertilizer—as well as the atrazine—will leach out into the surrounding waters, ultimately flowing to the Mississippi River and to the Gulf of Mexico. While the farmer reaps a profit when he sells his corn, he does not pay for the consequences of his fertilizer and pesticide run-off. Instead, the communities that sit downstream from his farm have to pay for water purification to remove the pollutants the farmer put in their water supply. The farmer also does not pay for the large dead zone in the Gulf that his runoff contributed to, nor does he assume responsibility for the fishermen who no longer have jobs because of his farming practices, or the towns that used to profit from fishing-related tourism.

In short, industrialized agriculture privatizes the commons. Our air, water, soil, and biodiversity belong to all of us. When our aquifers run out of water, we *all* run out of water, even if a single person or company used up most of the water. Similarly, when a species becomes extinct, we all lose that species, even if only one person profited by destroying that species' habitat. In addition, not only do people today lose that species, but so do all future generations. And who can say what role any one species plays in our world? Nature is infinitely complex; we don't always know exactly what niche a particular species fills in its ecosystem, but we do know that every species fills a unique role and that once that species is gone, all other species in that ecosystem (including humans) have to adapt in order to find a new equilibrium.

Sustainable agriculture, on the other hand, respects the commons. A sustainable farmer leaves the air, water, soil, and biodiversity no worse than he or she found them, and often in better shape. The life on a sustainable farm purifies the air and the water while building up the soil, and these processes require the involvement of an enormous number of species, from the smallest microbes to the cows that graze on the farm's pasture. A city living downstream from a sustainable farm will not have to use its tax dollars to clean up pollutants the sustainable farm put in its water supply, nor will it suffer a loss in tourism because pollution from the sustainable farm killed its fish. Future generations living on the land of a sustainable farm will share as much nutrient-rich soil as the people living on it today, if not more. The water will still be plentiful, the air will be clean, and the ability to produce food will not be limited or decreased because of the sustainable farm's actions in the present day.

Sustainable Farmers As Activists

As industrial agriculture has taken hold over the last fifty years, more and more people have come to realize that the system is not sustainable, in particular, the people who best understand the land—farmers. As a result, farmers have become some of the strongest proponents today for healthy food, thriving local economies and a clean environment—in short, a sustainable agricultural system.

John Peck serves as executive director of Family Farm Defenders, a group that promotes sustainable farming practices and is a staunch supporter of family farms. Upon hearing of my interest in food issues, in July 2006 John invited me to a meeting of the National Family Farm Council (NFFC) in Tomah, Wisconsin. When I heard that the itinerary would include a trip to a cranberry farm, I immediately agreed to attend.

During my visit to the Wetherby Cranberry Farm, I came to realize how intelligent and capable today's family farmers must be in order to survive in a world that prizes industrial growing methods.[3] Nodji Van Wychen, the owner of the farm, spoke in great detail about the proper soil required to grow cranberries, the pests to which cranberries are prone, and a variety of other topics which demonstrated her vast knowledge of biology. Later, as we moved indoors to view some of the equipment used in harvesting cranberries, she told us that since few companies find it profitable to manufacture the specialized equipment cranberry growers need to harvest and sort their berries, her farm had to construct its own machines. Wrapping up the tour, Nodji—connecting past to present—showed us several antique pieces of equipment from the early twentieth century that her farm still uses to sort the good berries from the bad. Finally, we were treated to a demonstration of the machine used to package the berries, which used bags of different sizes and featuring different logos, depending on where the cranberries were going to be sold. By the end of the tour, I realized that Nodji, in addition to displaying vast scientific and mechanical knowledge, had also mastered the entrepreneurial skills required to operate a small business and market her product.

Nodji was representative of many of the farmers I met at

the conference. And, in addition to their skills and knowledge of natural agricultural techniques, the farmers at the NFFC meeting also displayed significant political and economic acumen, reflecting the goals of the organization, which is to "empower family farmers by reducing the corporate control of agriculture and promoting a more socially just farm and food policy."[4] Because of their mission, the many farming groups that comprise the NFFC do not fight for family farms to preserve an old fashioned way of life; they fight to preserve quality of life for all people by "working together democratically to advance a food and agriculture system that ensures health, justice, and dignity for all."[5]

The NFFC is just one group of many that are leading the fight for sustainable agriculture. In this day and age, the fight has taken on a serious political dimension, as many of our current laws provide advantages to multinational corporations that work against sustainability or in some cases, even specifically outlaw sustainable practices. For example, there are laws that make it difficult for new farms to begin operation, as well as adding incentives that prevent unsustainable farms from converting to more sustainable techniques. Sometimes, particularly under the Bush administration, the government published information that was factually incorrect and then used that information as the basis for making rules or passing laws. Groups like the NFFC work to make sure our laws offer sustainable farmers a fair opportunity to make a living, which in turn assures that the rest of us are able to eat sustainably produced food.

A Growing Movement

In contrast to the unnatural and mechanistic practices of factory farms, farmers who engage in sustainable agriculture use the earth's resources, such as soil, minerals, energy and water to grow their crops and raise their animals. Some of the techniques used in sustainable food production include age-old methods such as crop rotation, use of beneficial insects, and diversification paired together with modern technology like scaring away pest birds with recordings of predatory bird calls and using microbiology to improve soil quality.

One farm that exemplifies the sustainable agriculture movement is located in Austin, Texas and is owned and operated by Judith McGeary, a former environmental lawyer, and her husband Mike, a retired military man. Their farm may be just a small patch of land in the center of a state better known for oil and feedlot beef, but it is an extremely healthy patch.

I visited the farm a week after their sheep had given birth, and watched in joy as the baby lambs head-butted their mothers enthusiastically and wagged their tails while they nursed. (Quite a difference from the way animals imprisoned on CAFOs act.) In addition to sheep, Judith and Mike also raise heritage breeds of turkeys, Bourbon Reds and Regal Reds. Many of the turkeys are escapees from Thanksgiving dinner, and are now living out long lives as a breeding flock. At dinnertime, Mike demonstrated how the turkeys eagerly followed him as he drove around in a golf cart distributing food (organic grain and sunflower seeds), gobbling every step of the way. At one point, a male turkey puffed up his feathers, looking like the craft projects first graders make by tracing their hands. I asked Judith if that meant "I'm impressive" or "I'm horny." The former, she said, although her turkeys spend much of their time with puffed up feathers when they are breeding. And, unlike the commercial breed of turkeys you find in supermarkets, the Broad Breasted White, the turkeys on Judith and Mike's farm are able to reproduce by themselves, without being artifically inseminated like commercial breeds.

Surprisingly, the most interesting animal on the farm was the dung beetle. As we crouched near the ground to avoid startling the sheep, Judith kicked over what I assumed was a pile of sheep manure, exposing an anthill. She explained that the dung beetles bury and consume the manure so there is nothing left but soil where the manure used to be. Thanks to the beetles and countless other organisms (most of them microscopic), the ground on Judith and Mike's farm feels like you are walking on well-padded plush carpeting. "When we bought the land," Judith told me, "it had just been fertilized and sprayed with pesticides. It was beautiful—lush and green—but there was no life larger than an insect." For the first two years after buying the farm, Judith sheepishly admits, she and Mike followed her neighbors' advice and used chemicals. Then they saw the light. Eight years after the last application of synthetic chemicals, the same land bursts with life. "Nothing fancy," Judith reflected, "But I see a wide variety of frogs, lizards, small mammals, and tons of birds."

The Miracle of Living Soil

One of the reasons that the soil at Judith and Mike's farm is so healthy is because they follow the teachings of Elaine Ingham, a Professor at Oregon State University and President and Director of Research at the Soil Foodweb Institute. Dr. Ingham leverages her vast knowledge of the soil food web to nourish plants and control pests. Her main belief is in the establishment of a healthy food web, which occurs when:

1. All the organisms the plant requires are present and functioning.
2. Nutrients in the soil are in the proper forms for the plant to take-up.
3. The correct ratio of fungi to bacteria is present, and ratio of predator to prey is present, so soil pH, soil structure, and nutrient cycling occur at the rates and produce the right forms of nutrients for the plant.[6]

For non-moving organisms, plants exert a surprising amount of control over the environment around them, choreographing microorganisms to obtain nutrients, as well as secreting "exudates" from their roots, which attract beneficial bacteria and fungi.[7] The bacteria and fungi then form a physical layer of defense against organisms harmful to the plant, and bind to soil particles to improve soil crumb structure. At the same time, they also attract nematodes and protozoa. The nematodes and protozoa dine on the bacteria and fungi, then excrete nutrients in forms that plants can use. Unlike fertilizer, which partially drains through the soil beyond where plants can use it, soil organisms immobilize nutrients, keeping them right where the plants need them.

To nurture the microscopic life in their soil, Judith and Mike apply compost teas, which are mixtures brewed up with high-quality compost to multiply the microorganisms within them. To this compost tea they then add organic fertilizers such as molasses and fish hydrolysate (basically, liquefied fish from fishing waste) to feed the microorganisms until the natural, symbiotic plant-microorganism relationship develops.

Because the nutrient requirements of plants can be as complex and individualized as those of people, Judith told me about a technology she and Mike are experimenting with. Before using an organic fertilizer, Judith first tests its effectiveness by applying it individually to a plant and then testing the plant's Brix score (a measurement of the plant's nutrient content) before and after application of the fertilizer. At the same time, she uses another plant sprayed with water as a control. A higher Brix score indicates a healthier plant, so if the fertilizer is successful, the plant's Brix score will rise more than the control plant's score. Judith also cited experiments in which the vines of two tomato plants were twisted together—one planted in potting soil, the other planted in rich compost—and aphids were released upon them. The bugs will prefer the plant in potting soil every time, she told me. This is because, in her words, "what's healthy for plants and humans is bad for insects and vice versa."

The Four Cycles of Nature
Beyond the theories of Dr. Ingham, life also thrives at Judith and

Mike's farm because of Allan Savory's concepts of healthy natural cycles—water, community dynamics, mineral and energy.[8] Savory grew up in Africa and, observing environmental degradation over the course of his lifetime, developed a system of holistic management that is applicable to all land, whether wild or cultivated by humans.

All four cycles hinge on soil quality. An efficient water cycle allows precipitation to seep deep into the soil, eventually reaching the groundwater. Plants then use the water from the soil, and the water returns to the air via transpiration from plants, not evaporation. For such a cycle to operate, however, the soil must contain adequate organic matter and feature a sufficient "crumb structure" that holds water through capillary action while also allowing it to penetrate deeper. When the soil surface becomes capped, water evaporates or runs off instead of soaking in where plants can use it and where it can accumulate over time. Since plants require aeration as well as water to grow, a lack of water in the soil harms them, as does standing water when the soil's capped surface cannot absorb precipitation.

When an efficient water cycle is achieved, organisms can weather floods and droughts better than they can in an inefficient cycle. When there is too much water present, the soil can absorb the excess into the groundwater, and when too little water is present, the soil can provide plants with stored moisture. In climates that feature dry seasons, plants begin growing earlier in the growing season because they can utilize the soil's stored water before receiving any new precipitation.

The second cycle in Savory's system, community dynamics, underscores the importance of biodiversity. In an environment with few species, outbreaks of disease, weeds, insects and rodents are common. However, when biodiversity increases, the stability of populations within that community also increases. Much of this diversity occurs underground, including bacteria, fungi, earthworms, nematodes, protozoa and plant roots. Savory notes that a healthy pasture where cattle graze can contain an earthworm population equal to twice the weight of the cattle. Once the number of species increases, so does the web of interdependence among them, helping each individual species survive variations in weather. One reason for the increased stability with increased complexity is the contribution of all of the species living in the soil, working together to break down decaying matter, aerate the soil and help the water, mineral and energy cycles continue effectively.

A healthy environment also features an effective mineral cycle. According to Savory, "a good mineral cycle implies a biologically active living soil with adequate aeration and energy underground to sustain an abundance of organisms that are in continuous contact with nitrogen, oxygen, and carbon from the atmosphere."[9] This cycle takes place as plants absorb nutrients from the soil, which are passed on to the animals that eat the plants and the animals that eat those animals. Plants and animals then return these minerals to the soil either via excretion, or when they die and decay. In an efficient mineral cycle, a rich population of microorganisms lives in the soil to break down dead plant and animal matter, recycling nutrients to travel through the cycle again. Once again, the ability of the cycle to continue depends on the health of the soil—if the soil isn't teeming with microorganisms, dead matter on the surface oxidizes instead of decaying, without returning minerals to the soil.

These three processes complement the energy cycle. All energy that sustains life originates with the sun, and plants have the unique ability to capture that energy and store it in a usable form that other creatures can consume. Herbivores and omnivores eat the plants and in turn, omnivores and carnivores eat them. At each stage, some energy is lost as heat. Ultimately, plants, the animals that ate the plants, and the animals that ate those animals all die and decay, providing energy for the organisms that break down their remains. The organic matter forms soil in which plants can grow, starting the cycle once again as plants convert sunlight into energy.

Since the energy cycle begins and ends in soil, healthy soil plays a crucial role in providing energy for all life on earth. Savory adds one more reason why healthy soil is essential to the energy cycle. In order to increase the amount of energy produced, one has to increase either the density of vegetation, the time during which it can grow (or rate of growth) or the surface area of individual leaves that convert sunlight to energy.[10] As noted before, an efficient water cycle can increase the amount of time that plants are able to grow. Savory describes three types of plants: those that thrive in wet ground with poor aeration; those that require a balance of air and water; and those that do best in dry climates. Of the three types of plants, the ones that prefer a balance of air and water in the soil tend to feature the broadest leaves and thereby perform the most photosynthesis. By managing soil so that it achieves an optimal balance of moisture and aeration, we can also produce the maximum amount of energy to sustain life.

Naturally, Savory's four cycles overlap one another; an environment in which one cycle is not functioning properly will most likely have problems with the other cycles as well. Savory's work on holistic management requires determining whether an environment is brittle (arid for most of the year) or non-brittle (humid for most of the year) and then using the right tools to optimize all four cycles. Even without understanding the differences between brittle and non-brittle environments or how one may use various tools to manage them, you should already understand the flaw in relying on pesticides and commercial fertilizers (or other hallmarks of industrialized agriculture, such as monoculture, growing only one crop over a large area). As biodiversity increases, the stability of individual populations increases as well. However, when most species are wiped out with a chemical application, the remaining species (or the ones that return soon) lack the balance they would have in a diverse ecosystem.

An anecdote I read in *Mother Earth News* demonstrated how Savory's cycles might occur in pesticide-free agriculture.[11] A farmer lost half his potato crop to pests during his first year of organic farming, but over time, numerous species of beneficial insects moved in to prey on the pests. Instead of relying on pesticides, the farmer used composted chicken manure and wood shavings, cover crops, and crop rotation, tactics that promoted biodiversity, beginning with the smallest microbes in the soil and on up the food chain from there.

Compare that example with the gymnastics strawberry growers in California go through to create sterile growing conditions.[12] First, they seal an entire field in plastic and inject a chemical called methyl bromide, a soil fumigant notable for its side effect of depleting the ozone layer. Instead of creating an environment where numerous species can thrive, bringing pest species into balance, the strawberry growers use this harmful pesticide to kill all life in the soil before planting their berries. After using the methyl bromide, they discard the plastic, install drip irrigation hoses, and cover the fields with new plastic, into which they insert the strawberry plants. At the end of the harvest, the plants, plastic, and hoses are thrown away. Keeping the natural world as sterile as a laboratory is obviously difficult and resource intensive—not to mention toxic! While farmers today are searching for a replacement for methyl bromide, which is being phased out internationally due to its effects on the ozone layer, the overall philosophy behind growing one type of crop over a large area in sterile soil remains largely unchanged.[13]

Healthy Animals, Healthy Environment
Another lesson I learned from Judith and Mike was how, in accordance with Savory's teaching, animals can contribute to the health of a farm. According to Savory, a brittle environment lacking grazing and animal impact will falter because the vegetation will die during the dry season, but the environment lacks the

organisms of decay to break the vegetation down. As a result, during the following growing season, the seeds will find have difficulty obtaining enough sunlight as the dead vegetation of the previous year stands in their way. With grazing animals present, the animals eat the vegetation, break it down internally, and excrete it as manure (eagerly awaited by dung beetles and other soil life). Savory emphasizes the importance of animal impact, which he describes as follows:

> I noted that while bunched as a herd animals stepped recklessly and even very coarse plants, containing much old material that would not be grazed or trampled normally, were trampled down. That provided cover for the soil surface. In addition, the hooves of bunching and milling animals left the soil chipped and broken. In effect, the animals did what any gardener would do to get seeds to grow: first loosen the sealed soil surface, then bury the seed slightly, compact the soil around the seed, then cover the surface with a mulch. I also noted that where the grazing herd had kept off the steep, cutting edges of gullies, the bunched herd now beat down the edges, creating a more gradual slope that could once again support vegetation."[14]

For the land to receive the animal impact it requires, the ecosystem must include either wild or domesticated grazing mammals. From sheep to turkeys to dung beetles, Judith and Mike's farm demonstrates the role that nature intended for animals to play in the various ecosystems—provided they are raised and treated in the way nature intended as well. The revelation that one can raise animals in a way that makes the environment healthier was just one of the many lessons I took away from Judith and Mike.

4. YES, I'VE HEARD THE ONE ABOUT 'WHOLE PAYCHECK'

As mainstream agriculture has adopted chemicals as a means of providing soil fertility and controlling pests, it has been left to people like Judith and Mike, who believe in working with nature (instead of trying to overpower it), to establish what is known as the "organic movement." Despite the claims of industrial agriculture, going organic does not mean sacrificing longterm productivity due to losses by pests. As we saw on Judith and Mike's farm, when grown in soil that is rich in bacteria, fungi, protozoa, and other organisms, plants are able generate their own resistance to pests. Furthermore, an environment rich in biodiversity stabilizes populations of individual species—pests included—as beneficial insects, birds, and bats move in to prey on pest species.

Consumers obtain many health benefits from organics, in particular increased nutrients and less harmful agricultural chemicals in their food. And, when consumers buy organic food from local family farmers, they are also promoting healthier communities and stimulating their local economies by establishing a one on one relationship between producer and buyer, a relationship that creates a level of trust about the quality of the food we eat.

In the United States, the phrase "certified organic" technically means following standards set by the USDA's national organics program and obtaining certification from an Accredited Certifying Agency (ACA). However, in a more general (and pure) sense, organic agriculture means producing food by working with nature instead of trying to overcome nature. Organics allow nature to do the heavy lifting, resulting in a higher quality product and a cleaner environment than food produced using industrial methods.

A terrific definition of organics is offered by the California Certified Organic Farmers:

> Organic food is produced by farmers who emphasize the use of renewable resources and the conservation of soil and water to enhance environmental quality for future generations (USDA).

> Certified organic food in the United States is grown according to standards set by the National Organic Program.

> According to those standards, organic food is produced without using most conventional pesticides; fertilizers made with synthetic ingredients or sewage sludge; bio-engineering; or ionizing radiation. Organic meat, poultry, eggs, and dairy products come from animals that are given no antibiotics or growth hormones. [1]

The father of U.S. organic standards is a man named Harry MacCormack.[2] Educated at Harvard, Harry, now in his mid-sixties, grew up in upstate New York, back when farming organically was known simply as "farming." Harry moved to California as a teenager, where he had two life-changing experiences that cemented his views as an advocate of organic agriculture. First, while working one summer picking beans, a crop duster flew overhead, spraying Harry and the migrant workers alongside him with DDT. Harry's understanding of chemical contamination in the environment deepened a few years later when his father learned that two solvents from his work at IBM had been found in the local water system. Harry worked with his father as they tried to clean up the mess, making discoveries about water contamination along the way. With such firsthand knowledge of pesticides' persistence in the environment, Harry had no intention of ever adopting "conventional" farming practices.

In 1984, Harry first codified organic standards in a document titled "The Standards and Guidelines for Organic Agriculture," which became the basis for many organic certification programs in the U.S. and abroad. Back in the 1980s, organic was still years away from becoming a household word, but the idea was starting to catch on behind the scenes—notably among large companies like Kellogg and Del Monte. While multinational corporations may not subscribe to the philosophy behind organic agriculture, they can spot an opportunity for profit where one exists, and organic food represented a new opportunity for them. As Harry put it, "They were willing to play by the rules if there were rules."

The road to government certification began in 1990, when Congress passed the Organic Foods Production Act (OFPA). The purpose of OFPA was to establish national standards for the production and handling of foods labeled as "organic." Prior to OFPA, private and state agencies were responsible for defining what was meant by organic. As a result, there were no consistent, across the board standards, which meant that organic could mean something entirely different depending on what state you were in, or who was responsible for the certification process. OFPA was designed to clear up this confusion, as well as to protect against mislabeling or fraud.[3]

The Organic Foods Production Act created the National Organic Standards Board (NOSB), which is responsible for advising the Secretary of Agriculture on setting standards for the USDA's National Organic Program. Currently, appointments to the NOSB are made by the Secretary for five year terms, and include among their members farmers, handlers/processors, retailers, scientists, consumer/public interest advocates and environmentalists.[4] Despite meager funding and a small staff, the National Organic Program operates by accrediting nearly 100 third-party accredited certifying agencies, who in turn provide the oversight required to certify farms and businesses as organic. Since the standards cover the materials and processes used for both growing and processing food, not only does NOP regulate which pesticides a farmer may use, it also specifies which cleaning solution a processor may use to clean his equipment.

Since I buy most of my food directly from the farm on which it was grown, I find it strange to eat something without knowing where it came from and who grew it. I realize this makes me a bit of a rarity in today's world—you should see the looks I get when I offer an orange to a friend, adding that it is a transitional organic, i.e. grown by a farmer who is pursuing organic certification but who is not yet officially certified. To most people, an orange is an orange is an orange. While the USDA organic certification process attempts to strike a middle ground between my desire to know exactly how my food was grown and the needs of a distribution system that separates producers and consumers by several middlemen, in order for the system to work effectively it must give me the assurance that the USDA organic seal means that someone asked the same questions I would ask if I could speak with the farmer or producer myself.

And what are these questions? When buying eggs, I ask the farmer how many chickens they own and if those chickens are on pasture. (One time when I asked those questions of a farmer at the market, his answers were "3,000" and "No," respectively. Needless to say I didn't buy eggs from him.) Additionally, instead of asking farmers whether they are certified organic, I will ask if they use sprays on their crops. If they say no, then I buy from them, even if they aren't certified organic (Because it costs money and takes time to achieve organic certification, some farmers choose not to get certified, even if they may meet or exceed USDA organic standards.) Once a strawberry grower smugly told me that methyl bromide was great stuff, so of course I didn't buy any strawberries from him.

To me, however, the best thing about buying directly from farms is the relationship you build with the individual farmers. For example, a farmer I buy oranges from once told me that the reason she went organic was so her young niece would be able to run out into the orchards and eat the fruit off her trees without worrying about what had been sprayed on them. As a result of this kind of intimate relationship between eater and grower, I know that "my" farmers, in addition to growing food in a way I find appealing, also have the same vision for our food system as I do.

All this isn't to say that organics are not without their problems. According to Harry MacCormack, the "Pandora's box" of organic farming is chemical residues that are left behind in the ground from previous, conventional farming practices. As an example, Harry told me that when one grows large crops that spend a long time on the field (like winter squash) in soil that contains trace amounts of DDT-relatives chlordane or dieldrin, these pesticides multiply four times in the squash flesh, and eight times in the squash seeds. Because of this, Harry's ACA, Oregon Tilth, won't certify farmers who grow squash or potatoes in contaminated soil, though nothing in the official organic standards actually forbids it. Harry feels that organic standards ought to be updated based on current pesticide uptake data.

Another problem with organics is the so-called 95/5 rule. Since food processing uses many chemicals for which no organic alternatives exist, organic processors often struggle to use 100 percent organic products. In 2005, Arthur Harvey, an organic blueberry farmer from Maine, won a lawsuit in which he charged that organic ought to mean 100 percent organic, not 95 percent organic and 5 percent or less synthetic (as processors were interpreting the law at the time). Faced with the choice of fighting the ruling or phasing out organic products that required some synthetic inputs, the Organic Trade Association cut a deal with members of the House that stated that USDA certified organic processed food must be 95 percent organic, with the remaining 5 percent coming from a list of 38 approved synthetic substances if the producer can prove that no organic alternative is available. Despite the compromise, Harry still feels that organic proponents came out ahead because the number of synthetics allowed has been narrowed down to 38, where before, organic food processors were using literally thousands of synthetic substances in their products. (Others disagree, wishing the list of 38 be reduced to 0, even if it means that many processed foods would no longer be certified organic.)

Overall, talking to Harry MacCormack reassured me that organics, despite their problems, set a high bar for those who want to be part of the system, ensuring that anyone wishing to tout organic certification for their product take the necessary precautions to keep synthetic chemicals out of them. Harry believes that when it comes to organics, the Unites States has "the best stuff outside of Europe." For consumers looking to avoid pesticide consumption, organics are a great way to go. Still, organics are currently less than 5 percent of the market, and much of it comes from the third world, where standards are lax. Harry would like to see us adopt a system that produces 20 to 30 percent of our food locally, with the eventual goal of working up to 50 percent. Until then, Harry says, "We have a warehousing and trucking system, we don't have a food system."

Industrial Ag Invades Organics

Whenever I hear the phrase "industrial organics," i.e. organic production on a large, industrial scale, I recall the section in *The Omnivore's Dilemma* when author Michael Pollan describes the mechanized process used at Greenway Organic to make the land weed-free. "The heavy tillage—," Pollan wrote, "heavier than in a conventional field—destroys the tilth of the soil and reduces its biological activity as surely as chemicals would."[5] Indeed, while organic certification denotes products grown or raised without most pesticides or commercial fertilizers, GMOs (genetically modified organisms), antibiotics, hormones or (my favorite) sewage sludge, it is not an overall measure of sustainability. For example, when a large producer learns to stick to the letter of the law with the intent of maximizing profit at the expense of the environment, the result is hardly an organic consumer's ideal. On this note, I find the lists of corporate ownership of major organic brands to be very telling. On the other hand, many sustainable operations do not pursue certification even though they fully adhere to organic standards. If you meet most of your customers face to face, you do not need to pay an ACA to inspect your farm—your customers will do that for you!

Parent Company[6]	Organic Brands
Kraft	Boca Foods Back to Nature
Pepsi	Naked Juice
General Mills	Cascadian Farm Muir Glen
Dean	Horizon The Organic Cow of Vermont Alta Dena White Wave/Silk
Conagra	Lightlife Alexia Foods
Cadbury Schweppes	Green & Black's

Parent Company[6]	Organic Brands
Kellogg	MorningstarFarms Natural Touch Kashi Gardenburger Bear Naked
Coca-Cola	Odwalla
M&M Mars	Seeds of Change
Hershey Foods	Dagoba

I don't make these points to critique the quality of certified organic food in stores like Whole Foods or Trader Joe's, whose shelves are filled with organic brands owned by enormous food companies. Organic standards set the bar at a certain level, and individual organic producers fall all over a wide range above that bar. My point is merely that when you do not purchase your food directly from a farmer, you cannot be sure where within that range of sustainability your food may fall. The only assurance you have is that it meets the bare minimum requirements, essentially promising only that you will avoid consuming most pesticides, GMOs, etc.

Working at Whole Foods

As a sustainable food aficionado, my attitude towards Whole Foods and other national chains offering organic food changes based on the available alternatives. When I can buy directly from local farmers and food artisans, I avoid places like Whole Foods. However, when I am on the road and my next best option is Subway, I look to Whole Foods as an oasis. After reading *The Omnivore's Dilemma's* harsh account of Whole Foods and its suppliers (Michael Pollan traces some of the food sold at Whole Foods back to its suppliers, and what he discovers is not necessarily the "supermarket pastoral" that the company promises) and then seeing Pollan debate Whole Foods CEO John Mackey, I decided to get to the bottom of the matter by taking a job in the bakery at the Whole Foods in San Diego. My goal was to answer the following question: Was Whole Food truly sustainable, or was it just a high-priced version of the same food one could find in a conventional supermarket?

Right off the bat, Whole Foods made an impressive effort to train its new staff members on how to properly handle organic food, as I, along with the rest of the new hires, had to complete an eight-week training course with team trainers before going before team and store managers to be quizzed on the information we had learned. In addition, we also had to complete computer based training on various topics (earning a free organic cotton T-shirt in the process). Even after our training was done, we had to submit to regular reviews by management from other stores in the region to prove that we were familiar with the correct procedures within our individual departments.

How well these procedures were followed by employees in the bakery varied widely. I, following the rules closely, occasionally had to decline customers' requests to slice their non-organic bread in our bread-slicing machine, as it was designated for organic use only. Likewise, certain spoons and pitchers were reserved exclusively for organics, which we had to wash in separate sinks from the dishes used for conventional food. While this might make it seem as if we were going to great lengths over minutia, to a customer who came to Whole Foods specifically because the store offered organics, accidentally mixing his organic latte with a few drops of conventional dish water would be a violation of his trust (and the law).

Overall, the bakery team leader and I were the most concerned about organics among the staff. Others, while less concerned about organic philosophy, were nevertheless competent and conscientious in doing their jobs. And then there were the few employees who didn't care at all. To Whole Foods credit, these employees were eventually fired, but I would speculate that a few organic customers had their dishes washed in the conventional sinks during those employees' time at the store.

Whole Food and the Locavore Movement

During my time behind the bakery counter, I came to learn that the Whole Foods customer base is not the eco-conscious yoga-addicted crowd one might infer by walking through a store. Many customers were interested in organics, and a large percentage also cared about their health. But did they care about buying local? No doubt some did, but it wasn't an issue I heard brought up more than a few times among the customers I served.

The store itself actively sought local products, even inviting local farmers to gather in the parking lot and share their products with customers. In addition, the store proudly displayed orange "local" signs (local being defined as "within San Diego County") wherever it could, with oranges, avocadoes, blackberries, strawberries, gelato, and rugelach cookies just a few of the items that earned such signs. Other signs profiled a number of local businesses and farms that supplied the store.

One day, about thirty customers and I piled into a bus that Whole Foods had chartered to take us to meet their local suppliers. We visited three farms on our trip—Stehly Farms Organics, Bella Vado, and Tierra Miguel. The first stop, Stehly Farms, was a 300 acre farm that grew organic avocados, citrus, and blackberries. Only about an hour outside San Diego, it was truly local. At the farm, we dined on fresh squeezed orange juice and guacamole while Noel, our host, told us the history of his farm. He also pointed out the solar panels that reduced his electric bills drastically and a mountain of chicken manure he had obtained for use as fertilizer. Later in the year, I had the opportunity to try the blackberries from Stehly Farms, verifying that Noel's claims about them were all true: they were enormous and juicy. Interestingly, on a later trip to Arizona, I discovered Stehly blackberries in the Paradise Valley Whole Foods. It seems that Whole Foods, while highlighting the local products in each location, also distributes some of those products regionally.

Of the three places we visited, only Stehly was an actual supplier for Whole Foods. At our second stop, Bella Vado, we watched a machine imported from Italy transform ripe avocados into avocado oil. At the time, Whole Foods had committed to selling Bella Vado's avocado oils in its stores, a promise it made good on less than a year later.

Unlike Bella Vado, our final destination, Tierra Miguel, was not on the fast track to becoming a Whole Foods supplier. Tierra Miguel's eighty-seven acres were lovingly tended in line with all of the organic and sustainable principles I had learned from Judith and Mike and other farmers who had taken the time to educate me. The farm operates a CSA (Community Supported Agriculture) program, in which members pre-pay in exchange for regular boxes of produce. Because of this, Tierra Miguel's first priority is supplying food to their members, and any future relationship with Whole Foods will occur only if they grow more than they need for their CSA program.

The True Believers

During lunch at Tierra Miguel, I chatted with Carolyn Kates, the marketing guru behind the field trip. Carolyn is a retired hospice nurse who works at Whole Foods because she enjoys the work and believes that Whole Foods has a positive impact on our food system. During my first week in the bakery, the warmth in her eyes and smile immediately drew me to her, and I know she must have been a tremendous comfort to her dying patients and their families during her career in nursing. Although every Whole Foods employee works to increase the store's profits (and thus increase their own paychecks through the company's gainsharing program), I believe that Carolyn promotes local products for more noble reasons as well. She is one of the many people I met while working at Whole Foods who I would classify as "true believers"—employees who seek to make the food system more sustainable through their work.

Unfortunately, the true believers do not have enough pull to transform Whole Foods as much as they would like to. For example, in the aftermath of the faux farmers' market in the parking lot, the management and marketing team at my store became determined to sell local, organic strawberries. I became aware of this effort when a local food activist came past my gelato counter one day, offering customers and employees a taste of the berries and recording our reactions as he went along. The berries were the real deal, not the red, Styrofoam balls so many Americans have become accustomed to getting from their local supermarket. I eagerly ate as many samples as I could, then took a few extra berries to garnish the strawberry gelato in the display case. I also bought a few pints of the berries once they became available for sale in the store, ignoring the high price tag because I wanted the store to recognize that there was in fact a demand for local food.

Despite my efforts, the strawberries disappeared as quickly as they had come, and I soon ran into the same food activist, who was now grumbling about the situation. While the store had paid to advertise their strawberries in an Earth Day brochure, the produce manager had now decided not to order any more of the local berries. I was friendly with the produce manager, so I asked him what had happened. He told me it was a simple business decision—he could not get the berries for a low enough price to sell them at an amount that people would pay. In addition, the berries the store received were so ripe that they barely lasted to the end of the day. While those berries would be in high demand at a farmers' market, where consumers buy their fresh produce over the course of a few hours, they were unsuited to the normal, industrialized food distribution chain.

Another true believer was Dennis, my manager in the bakery department. Although he first struck me as laid-back guy with a sense of humor, he had a serious side to him that included a strong belief in sustainable food. As a result, within our bakery, both the coffee bar and the hearth breads (the breads baked in the store) were 100 percent organic. An all-organic coffee bar is rare for Whole Foods since it requires extra sinks so the dishes reserved for organics can be washed separately, but Dennis made it happen by augmenting our regular sinks with a bucket of sanitizer reserved for organics. Dennis wanted to do a lot more—his dream was an all-organic bakery—but when he went head to head with regional management, he lost. Ultimately, feeling the stress of trying to improve the bakery with his hands tied by management, Dennis stepped down as manager.

Even after Dennis left, the bakery continued to add locally produced items to its inventory. Instead of serving gelato from Los Angeles, we began serving gelato from Coronado, just off the coast of San Diego. We also bought tea from a local business, Café Moto, and some of our bread from Julian, a town about an hour away. Several times a week, a man from Chewy's, a local rugelach business, stopped by to fill up the bins with rugelach. When he arrived, the cake decorators, Vicky and Josefina, were already at the end of their shifts, as they worked through the wee hours of the morning meticulously decorating the cakes and fruit tarts. Most of the cakes came from Sugar Plum Fairy in Gardena, 116 miles away, and Perfectly Sweet in Alhambra, 119 miles away. While these companies are relatively local to San Diego—and even closer to the Los Angeles Whole Foods—since, as we saw with Stehly Farms, much of Whole Foods distribution is organized regionally, this meant that the Phoenix stores, 350 miles away, also received the same cakes. An even less local supplier was Galaxy Desserts, which was located near San Francisco, about 500 miles away. I have enjoyed their lava cakes in San Diego—and at a Whole Foods in Dallas where I also found Chewy's rugelach. Conversely, I recently saw sticky toffee pudding that I had originally encountered at an Austin, Texas farmers' market for sale in the San Diego Whole Foods.

Overall, while Whole Foods plays up its relationship to local suppliers, the "local" products you buy are often from national companies that sell to Whole Foods' stores all over the country. While this doesn't negate the fact that your local purchases reduce the amount of oil used to bring the food to you, it does take away from the idea that you're supporting a small, local business. While Whole Foods has responded to the locavore movement to some extent, their response is driven in many ways more by marketing than by a true philosophical bent.

A Rind is a Terrible Thing to Waste

Another inescapable observation from my work at Whole Foods was the amount of food the store wasted. To be fair, wasted really isn't the right word, as the San Diego Whole Foods had a fantastic compost program, and all of the food we threw out was reincarnated in bags of Whole Foods compost bearing the slogan "Because a rind is a terrible thing to waste." Whole Foods should absolutely be commended for their commitment to the environment—and their very good business sense—for turning their waste into profitable compost. In my opinion, every other grocery chain should follow suit.

That said, the energy and packaging material required to produce and ship food is wasted when that food goes right into the compost bin. Each night, our bakery filled several shopping carts with spoilage—food that had reached its sell-by date, most of which was still perfectly fine to eat. Pastries and hearth breads, for example, were baked and sold on the same day, and any leftovers were considered spoilage. While a shelter picked up the hearth breads, it was the only item that escaped the compost bin, as we were told that we couldn't give food away for "liability" reasons, and that we could also not take food home ourselves because management was afraid that we would create extra spoilage to guarantee ourselves free food. Whenever I could, I would sneak out a bag of day-old pastries and give them to the homeless people in Balboa Park. I would also keep an eye out for products with an expiration date a few days away—while they were still "fresh," I'd give them out as free samples so that we wouldn't have to compost them later in the week.

The alternative to the volume of wasted food is, of course, ordering less food. However, buying the right amount of food is a fine line to walk, and often (especially in the case of newly introduced products) there is no way to predict sales. In addition, our bakery didn't carry foods that contained artificial preservatives, so our products' shelf lives were shorter than those in conventional supermarkets. And, whenever we ran out of a particular item, customers became absolutely indignant. Time and time again, I would put on a heavy jacket and dig through box after box in the walk-in freezer to look for a particular item someone wanted, as Whole Foods customers expect to get what they want, when they want it. They might care about environmental causes, but unless they've worked in a grocery store, they probably have no idea how much waste their demand for all foods to be available at all times creates.

The flip side is that the customers at Whole Foods pay high prices, which perhaps gives them license to be demanding. (My recent Whole Foods purchase of coffee, three mini chocolate bars, a six-pack of beer, and a ready-to-eat package of falafel ran me nearly $30.) A more savvy customer might carefully select only the Every Day Value items, which are priced more affordably, but the on the whole, the budget conscious aren't Whole Foods' customer base. (I was frequently asked if I'd heard the joke about the "Whole Paycheck." Oh yes, I've heard it.)

But what I finally realized while working at Whole Foods was that it's not that high quality organic food is a luxury reserved for the elite—it's that insisting on buying that type of food through unsustainable, conventional channels like supermarkets is such a luxury.

The Overall Verdict

My time at Whole Foods taught me that the same quality (and in many cases better) food can be obtained a little less conveniently and certainly for less money by purchasing directly from local farmers, shopping at farmers' markets, joining a CSA, or even growing your own garden. You might have to adjust your schedule to shop during market hours, and you won't be able to find all foods during all seasons, but you'll also have more control over how your food was produced, who your food dollars support, and how much oil was used to bring the food to you. Unlike when you shop at a grocery store, you won't be sending your money to far off middlemen, executives, or shareholders. When you buy from local farmers, your money will enrich the community you live in.

Despite its problems, Whole Foods still deserves a place on your shopping list when more sustainable options are unavailable, like during the winter months if your local farms and gardens are under several inches of snow. And shopping at Whole Foods is certainly infinitely preferable to buying from conventional grocery stores that, while selling food for less money, charge an even higher price than Whole Foods by operating their stores on non-renewable energy (Whole Foods uses wind power) and profiting from foods which unleash much harsher effects on the environment and on customers' health. Overall, when more sustainable options aren't available and I have no choice but to go to the grocery store, I prefer paying the higher prices at Whole Foods instead of paying in increased pollution somewhere else.

5. LIVING LA VIDA LOCAVORE

On November 18, 2007, the Rev. Dr. Arvid Straube, lead minister of the First Unitarian Universalist Church of San Diego, delivered a Thanksgiving sermon called "Eat, Love, and Prayer—Making the Most of Thanksgiving."[1] In talking about the consequences that are reaped by eating food that is produced by a system based on the exploitation of workers, animals and the land, Rev. Straube alluded to a phrase that Michael Pollan coined in *The Omnivore's Dilemma*, saying that Americans are suffering from a "national eating disorder." To counter this condition, Straube prescribed the advice of Alice Waters, the legendary founder of the restaurant Chez Panisse and a leader in the Slow Food movement:

> "First, eat sustainably and locally. Second, eat season-
> ally. You know think about how much energy is wasted
> and how much is contributed to global warming to fly
> cherries in from Chile in December. It just doesn't make
> sense. Shop at farmers' markets. Plant a garden. Con-
> serve. Compost. Recycle. Cook simply. Good, fresh,
> seasonal ingredients don't need a lot of stuff added, the
> taste is good on its own. Cook simply. Cook together.
> Eat together. Again, we've gotten to the point where

families eat very few meals together because of our hurry sickness. And it has been proven with many a study that families who eat together a lot are closer and have fewer problems. Eat together. And remember, this is the one I want to emphasize, remember food is precious."

While Waters is seen as a pioneer in the contemporary movement towards local, sustainable, healthy and socially responsible food, the concepts she espouses have in fact existed since the dawn of industrialized civilization. (I often think that, somewhere in America, there must be people who eat sustainably without considering themselves as part of a movement.) The rest of us, however, are finally waking up to the idea that there is an alternative to shrink-wrapped packaging and drive-thru windows. Apparently, as the sermon by Rev. Straube indicates, our lack of satiation from the food we eat runs so deep that we are starting to feel it as a spiritual hunger as well.

This chapter will introduce several local food movements and institutions whose collective goal is to "make all aspects of our food system—from production to consumption—healthier for people and the planet."[2] Since the modern food movement cannot be defined in a sentence or two—as author Marion Nestle puts it, "the movement does not seem to be organized in any visible way and is composed of many separate mini-and not-so-mini-movements that have developed independently"[3]—it is impossible for us to address the myriad problems in our food system in one simple, comprehensive movement or campaign. Rather, the drive toward sustainable, healthy food is comprised of various groups and worldviews, which, because of their shared goals, tend to overlap one another.

Farmers' Markets

Farmers' markets are often the first place where foodies-to-be interact with local food and discover the possibilities that exist outside the conventional grocery store. My introduction to the world of local food was at the Dane County Farmers' Market in Madison, Wisconsin. At first, I treated going to the market as a social opportunity, as my friends and I would meet up to walk around the Capitol square, sipping coffee and sampling the food. Over time, going to the farmers' market transitioned from an occasional social event to my main source of purchasing food. And once I got to know the farmers who grew my food—chatting them up about their growing methods, even on occasion visiting their farms—I found that I just couldn't go back to buying food from the grocery store.

According to the numbers, I'm in good company as a devotee of farmers' markets. The USDA began tracking farmers markets in 1994, when there were only 1,755 of them in the United States; that number had more than doubled by 2008, to 4,685.[4] While most Americans (57.7 percent) still buy their food at conventional supermarkets, and a growing percentage (17.9 percent) shop for their groceries at supercenters like Wal-Mart, two percent of Americans now report farmers markets as their main venue for food shopping.[5]

Farmers' markets vary by size, frequency (once a week, twice a week, etc.), location, whether they remain open during the winter, and by what food can be sold at the market and who can sell it. Naturally, the best markets are located in a convenient, central place, with ample parking and perhaps even bike racks, so that they can be easily patronized by farmers and customers. They should also be open when people are best able to shop (after work or on weekends) and ideally should stay open year round, moving indoors in the winter when the weather gets cold. In addition, the market should establish reasonable rules about what kind of food can be sold (for example, vendors shouldn't be allowed to buy produce at a chain like Costco and then sell it at the market). Finally, a good farmers' market should have enough vendors to provide eaters with a variety of food choices so that there is minimal need to supplement shopping at the market with a trip to the grocery store. I also prefer it when vendors at a market sell food produced with organic methods, although I don't mind if they are not certified organic.

The Dane County Farmer's Market meets all the standards listed above. The market requires that vendors only sell food they produce themselves (it's the largest producers-only market in the country) and it only allows vendors from within the state of Wisconsin. The furthest any food travels to reach the market are cherries from Door County, Wisconsin, about 200 miles away. While the vendors aren't all certified organic, nor do they all use organic methods, the Dane County Market is large enough so that organic shoppers never miss out on a food they desire because an organic option is unavailable.

The outdoor market begins every year in April, opening with very little in the way of fresh produce—mostly spinach and rhubarb—but with a reasonable variety that includes cheeses, meats, eggs, honey, maple syrup, jams, pickled vegetables, herbal tea, flour, baked goods and pasta. From May until early November, a parade of fruits and vegetables appear one by one at the market, every Saturday and Wednesday morning, reaching a peak in mid to late summer when nearly every form of produce under the sun is available. In the fall, the market remains in full swing—though hints of the end of the growing season are beginning to appear— with apples, winter squash, and brussel sprouts. (When the brussel sprouts were ripe, I knew that only a few precious weeks of the outdoor market remained.)

Around the middle of November, the market moves indoors. Despite the bitter Wisconsin winter, a surprising variety of fruits and vegetables are offered at the indoor market, including root vegetables, potatoes, apples and even some greens. But the best part of the winter market isn't the food you take home—it's the breakfast you eat while you are there. Each week, the market invites a local chef to create a breakfast menu made from locally produced foods. The last time I visited, I dined on apple raspberry crepes with maple syrup, apple cider and locally roasted coffee. (Being a vegetarian, I skipped the bacon.)

In addition to offering locally produced food, farmers' markets also provide a community connection between eaters and growers. When you shop regularly at a farmers' market, you become well-acquainted with the individual farmers, their personalities, their products and their growing methods. In Wisconsin, for example, when buying potatoes, I became a loyal customer of Driftless Organics after I asked the farmer which variety of potatoes I should use for a soup and he recommended his German butterballs. The potatoes—and the soup—were amazing and I never bought potatoes from anyone else as long as I lived in Madison. In San Diego, I enjoy visiting the table of La Milpa Organica, a small organic farm in Escondido, where I can always expect to encounter new herbs or greens I've never seen before. Sometimes, they have such strange varieties of familiar plants that I have to ask what they are, like when they offered yellow cucumbers, Bordeaux red-stemmed spinach or giant okra.

On the flipside, shopping at the farmers' market also allows you to discover which farmers to avoid, like the strawberry vendor I mentioned in the previous chapter who insisted that methyl bromide was a fantastic chemical to use for growing strawberries. But whether your discoveries about a particular vendor are for better or worse, the kind of intimate information you obtain about your food—and the people who grow it—at a farmers' market is a world apart from what you learn from a label on a can at the grocery store.

Local and Sustainable Food in Restaurants

These days, it is not only consumers who are buying more of their food directly from local farmers; restaurant chefs are also getting involved in the local, sustainable food movement. Founded in 1993, the Chefs Collaborative came together to "work with chefs and the greater food community to celebrate local foods and foster a more sustainable food supply."[6] The goal of the Collaborative is to provide its membership—70 percent of whom are chefs—with the tools to run "economically healthy, sustainable food service businesses." Members of the Collaborative work together to help ensure that restaurants use the "highest-quality, best-tasting local ingredients," so that the food they serve is healthy for people, good for the environment, and has a positive impact on local communities. In addition to the Collaborative, there are also many other restaurants across the country that, while focusing less on local food, emphasize other aspects of sustainability, for example committing to serve organic fare and pasture-raised meat. As an eater, I am grateful that more and more restaurants are beginning to share my preference for local, sustainable food. Who knew that "activism" could be so delicious!

Many cities boast restaurants that specialize in local food, from the most famous, like Chez Panisse in Berkeley, L'Etoile in Madison, and Blue Hill in New York, to lesser known but equally quality establishments including Rx in Philadelphia and Café Pasqual's in Santa Fe. Even Barack Obama enjoys dining on local food when he visits Topolobampo in Chicago. I'm grateful that my favorite locavore restaurant happens to be located in the city where I live—a vegetarian restaurant named Spread, in San Diego's North Park neighborhood.

Unless you are looking for it, you probably wouldn't even notice Spread, as the restaurant's muted lighting and unremarkable appearance pale in comparison to the flashy theatre located on the same block. Yet Spread attracts a steady stream of business, and does so without advertising—that is how loudly its food appeals to diners, inspiring them to come back over and over again to "spread" the word.

A food delivery truck has never pulled up to the front entrance of Spread.[7] Instead, each morning, owners Andrew and Robin Schiff wake up at 5:30 to begin gathering the ingredients for that evening's menu. The belief that "the moment you pull [a food] from the vine, that's the moment it's supposed to be eaten" drives Andrew to search for ingredients from farms and farmers' markets as distant as Temecula, about 75 miles away. He and Robin personally select each day's ingredients, sometimes picking the vegetables themselves. "A lot of times," Robin told me, "We're out there fighting off ducks for beets." By 4:00 in the afternoon, it's time for Robin and Andrew to head home for a quick shower in order to make it to the restaurant by 5:00, where they will design that evening's menu from their chosen ingredients, write it out on a large chalkboard (they avoid using disposable products like paper menus), and then open the doors at 6:00 p.m.

On the day I was talking with Andrew about the restaurant, Robin burst in the door carrying a bundle that included kaffir lime leaves. I had a notepad and pencil, ready to ask about the more mundane details of the business, but Robin's focus was only on the food; she had a little under an hour to turn the ingredients she was carrying into a menu, which that evening would feature a Thai vegetable pizza topped with heirloom vegetables and a black sesame reduction, two salads, rosemary and citron-scented edamame, olive oil and shallot crusted purple potato tacos, a lavender tart, and a kaffir lime and kumquat glazed vegetable mix. As she put it, "it's so much more interesting to not fall back on fat for flavor."

While Robin and Andrew view their cooking as a nightly "free form art extravaganza," in fact, their impact on San Diego reaches beyond merely tantalizing diners' palates with a new, local menu each night. They've also formed relationships with local farmers, thus helping to economically enrich the city's organic agricultural community. In return for Spread's business, farmers work with Andrew and Robin when planning their planting, growing varieties of heirloom vegetables specifically for use in the restaurant. Andrew sees this as "supporting mom 'n pop businesses [and] bringing identity back to the American landscape."

Despite the high quality of its food, eating at Spread is a dining experience that I reserve for special occasions, as once one factors in the true cost of local food plus gourmet preparation and excellent customer service, the price winds up being more than I—as well as most people—can afford on a regular basis. (Then again, the prices at Spread are no higher than those at your average high-end steakhouse, and the food is of infinitely better quality.) Unfortunately, as Bee Wilson pointed out in *The New Yorker*: "cheap food can be nasty, not to mention bad for farmers and the environment. Yet it has one great advantage . . . people can afford to buy it."[8]

However, in reality, cheaper food does not have to necessarily mean nasty food. At a restaurant called Roots Kind Food, three women are working to make local, organic food accessible and affordable to all. Roots Kind Food operates out of a small kiosk on Newport Street, the main drag of San Diego's Ocean Beach community, serving vegetarian wraps, salads, and sandwiches. When I sat down to chat with one of the owners, Heather Weightman, I realized how lucky her customers are, as Heather is a registered dietitian, with a master's in public health to boot. Probably the only other place most people eat food prepared by someone so well-educated about nutrition is in the hospital, and I doubt that many hospitals serve Thai peanut wraps garnished with edible flowers.

Just like Spread, Roots was founded with a social mission in mind. The idea came about when Heather moved with her husband to Pennsylvania. While he found a good job, she struggled to find her niche. Perhaps she could open a vegetarian restaurant, she thought. When Heather told her sister, Danielle Summerville, about her idea, Danielle encouraged her to move home to San Diego so they could start the restaurant together. After a few years of planning and an invitation to their friend Jaime Reed to join them, Roots became a reality: a vegetarian restaurant serving fresh, healthy, tasty food at an affordable price.

When I spoke with Heather in 2008, the food at Roots was about 50 percent organic and 15 percent local. She noted that they were still in their first year of business, and were gradually increasing their percentages of local and organic foods while working to maintain modest profitability and keep prices in the same range as other Ocean Beach eateries—a challenge in an era of rising food prices. Heather also told me that they are committed to using compostable to-go containers, silverware and cups.

While I have encountered a handful of lower priced restaurants that offer organic, local cuisine like Roots Kind Food—Urth Caffe in Los Angeles, for example—for the most part, local food has only proven to be a successful niche for celebrity chefs and high-priced restaurants. Sadly, it is difficult to succeed at a lower price level when you are competing against bakery cafes like Panera and your customer base doesn't always understand the value of choosing organic, local food.

Community Supported Agriculture

While buying food at a farmers' market or dining at a restaurant like Spread are the easiest and most pleasurable forms of food activism, participating in a CSA requires greater coordination and effort. Community Supported Agriculture originally started in Japan, migrating to the United States in the late 1980s. CSAs allow communities to share risk with their local farms by buying shares in the farm in exchange for receiving a corresponding share of what the farm grows.

For farmers, participating in a CSA makes good business sense, as it provides them with a degree of economic certainty; farmers receive money from their customers at the beginning of the growing season—when they need it most—and can then better plan out what to grow because there are now a specific number of people who will purchase their yield. As a customer, however, participating in a CSA can be a bit of a gamble, as you are taking the chance that you will like the food you receive from the farm, that you will be able to cook and eat that food in a timely fashion (or preserve it by canning or drying it) and that a natural disaster won't befall the farm you signed up with. To mitigate this risk, a CSA farm will usually let you know in advance what crops they are going to plant and when those crops will be harvested. And, in most years, Mother Nature won't send a disaster so great that your entire share of food will be lost. Another way the CSA model manages risk is if one crop gets wiped out (by a pest, for example), other crops will often produce in unexpectedly great numbers. As for your ability to cook and eat all of the food—that part is up to you!

The best CSA I have visited is a cooperative of several Amish farms in Lancaster County, Pennsylvania.[9] The cooperative originally came together in 2006, starting out with seven families. Three of the member farms had each run CSAs in the past, so when the new cooperative formed, it immediately acquired the 100 CSA customers from those farms.

The greatest challenge the cooperation faced during its first year in operation was poor coordination among the member farms to ensure that the variety and quantity of crops grown matched demand. To avoid that problem in the future, the cooperation planned for each farm to grow several crops (instead of every farm growing every crop), matching supply and demand, maximizing efficiency and also minimizing risk. This plan worked, as from seven families in 2006, the cooperation grew to twenty-five families in 2007 and forty in 2008. (They expect to grow to sixty families in 2009.) In addition, from 100 CSA customers in 2006, they anticipate growth to 1,000 in 2009. And, because the original seven farms were all organic, farms who are interested in joining the cooperation often go organic themselves, giving up their puppy mills and improving the living conditions of their livestock in order to qualify as new members.

In addition to the cooperative model, individual farms can also operate CSAs. As a person interesting in eating high-quality food, I have enjoyed being a member of a CSA run by a single farm; however, as an activist interested in the growth of the sustainable food movement, I prefer the cooperative model because it is scalable. Once a successful cooperative is established, other farms can join, and the CSA program can continue to grow without exposing farmers to the type of risk they might face by starting up their own CSA. I also like the cooperative as an incentive program to help new farms transition to organic means and otherwise increase their farms' sustainability. A cooperative also allows farmers to pool the cost, time and talent required to market a CSA, manage the financial aspect of the business, as well as store, pack and distribute food. Also, a cooperative decreases the risk for the consumer that a natural disaster will ruin an entire year's crop. While one farm may be damaged or destroyed, if the other member farms aren't affected, the CSA customers will be minimally impacted.

Finally, I have found that one of the most helpful features of belonging to a CSA is the newsletter that many provide to their customers containing recipes that use that particular week's foods. With a cooperative in place, farms can more easily combine their resources to provide weekly newsletters with recipes, ensuring that customers get the most from their CSA experience.

Slow Food

Another way to celebrate local cuisine is by getting involved with Slow Food International, an organization started in 1989 to "counteract fast food and fast life, the disappearance of local food traditions and people's dwindling interest in the food they eat, where it comes from, how it tastes and how our food choices affect the rest of the world."[10] Slow Food currently boasts 170 Chapters (called convivia) in the United States, as well as more than 100,000 members worldwide, spread among 132 countries.

In 2008, the organization held its first American national convention, Slow Food Nation, which drew 85,000 people to San Francisco over Labor Day weekend.

In addition to highlighting the value of eating "good, clean, fair food" and supporting local food producers, Slow Food seeks to educate its followers about the various intricacies that give unique flavor to food. At Slow Food Nation, for example, one could visit "Taste Pavilions" to sample bread, beer, wine, spirits, charcuterie, chocolate, honey, preserves, cheese, ice cream, fish, coffee, olive oil, native foods, pickles, chutney and tea. Similar to wine tastings at a vineyard, where you can learn about the variety of grapes used for a specific wine, why the region's climate and soil is ideal for growing those grapes and how the specific grape variety and other factors influence the taste of the wine, visitors to the Taste Pavilions were able to discover how differences in plant or animal variety, production method and other elements influence food flavor. To augment the Pavilions, "Taste Workshops" offered similar information in a classroom setting, with each workshop covering a specific topic like raw milk cheeses or the flavors native to a particular region of the United States.

One of the criticisms of Slow Food is that it is elitist, and yes, it is hard to ignore the high price tag of many Slow Food events. Despite this, Slow Food International provides an important service by focusing attention on local food and bringing together those who enjoy (and can afford) it. And those of us who cannot afford to dine in four star restaurants can still appreciate the business Slow Food brings to local farmers, as we all benefit from the positive environmental impact of eating food that is grown by farmers who respect the earth and promote biodiversity. I would be more critical of Slow Food for "elitism" if it were the only game in town, but fortunately the sustainable food movement is large, decentralized and growing, meaning there is something for everybody, even if Slow Food isn't your cup of tea.

Community Gardens and Urban Farms

Community gardens are parcels of land, often owned by non-profits or the government, that provide gardening opportunities to those who don't have the space to garden at home (generally urban dwellers). The gardens are usually divided into individual plots, with each plot tended by a different person or family. Many community gardens are so popular that they have long waiting lists. In light of skyrocketing food prices, *ABC News* did a story in 2008 on people who were saving money by growing their own food, citing increased demand for community gardens across the nation.[11] With the economy continuing to decline, 2009 was another banner year for gardens of all types, including community gardens.

Like community gardens, urban farms provide opportunities for city or suburban residents to engage in agricultural activities. However, unlike community gardens, an urban farm is more of a true farm operation, not just a patch of land where individuals can garden on their own plots. One of the best examples of an urban farm is Growing Power, which was started in Milwaukee in 1993 by Will Allen, a former professional basketball player. Today, Growing Power serves as an example of the possibilities of urban agriculture, with several sites in the greater Milwaukee area and in Chicago. A core aspect of Growing Power is the involvement of young people. From the start, the farm's mission was not only to grow food but to fight racism by organizing "people whose voices are rarely heard."[12] Growing Power also produces real food for poor neighborhoods that would otherwise be food deserts. On its initial two acres, Growing Power now has six greenhouses and three hoophouses full of plants, fish, bees, chickens, ducks, goats, rabbits and turkeys. The organization also runs a large composting operation, and uses an anaerobic digester to produce energy from food waste.

While urban agriculture is probably not the sole answer to the world's food problems, for those who enjoy growing their own food but lack the space to do so, it is a godsend. Even if urban agriculture alone cannot feed our cities, it still plays a vital role in bringing fresh, healthy food to areas that might not otherwise have any, as well as training the next generation of farmers and gardeners.

School Gardens

In a school garden, children can learn about biology and nutrition in a hands-on, fun way while simultaneously growing food for their school cafeteria or selling food to make money for their school (thus learning business skills). At the same time, they can also reduce the amount of trash from their school that goes to the landfill if it composts lunchroom waste. Today, school gardens are thriving across the country, from elementary schools to universities.

Perhaps the most famous school garden is Alice Waters' Edible Schoolyard at the Martin Luther King Jr. Middle School in Berkeley, California. The school began cultivating its one acre garden and utilizing its kitchen classroom in 1997, eventually becoming the subject of Water's book *Edible Schoolyard: A Universal Idea*, which "instructs children not only in academic lessons, but also teaches crucial life skills and builds self-esteem, all of which engenders cooperation and understanding amongst the participants. The garden also produces food that feeds all the attending students, ensuring that no child goes hungry."[13] While some schools struggle to offer school gardens because their states' growing season does not correspond well with the school year, California, because of its temperate Mediterranean climate and the leadership of influential figures like First Lady Maria Shriver, has seen its school gardens double over the past five years, to over 6,000.[14]

Farm to School

The farm to school movement developed as a logical marriage

between the desire to improve school lunch programs and the campaign to promote local food. By including fresh, local food in children's lunches, we are supporting local farmers as well as providing nourishment to children, hopefully providing them with the tools to maintain good eating habits for life. Currently, there are farm to school programs in forty states, covering over 8,700 schools.[15]

I asked Debra Eschmeyer, an organic farmer and the Program Media and Marketing Advisor to the National Farm to School Program, if she had a favorite farm to school program. "Each farm to school program is amazing and unique in its own way," she said. Elaborating, she added, "Whether started by a parent who cared about what her child was eating, or a teacher who was passionate about nutrition, or a farmer who wanted to sell food to the school, farm to school epitomizes the grassroots food movement for good food. It's the democratic food system at its best—these programs are formed by their communities and they enjoy the delicious fruits of their labor."

As Debra's words clearly show, each one of the over 2,000 farm to school programs that are currently active in American schools grew out of the needs of its particular community. It takes little imagination to understand why a farm to school program in southern California, where crops grow year round, would be very different from a program in upstate New York, where the growing season is shorter. And naturally, schools differ in other ways, from the availability of funding and kitchen equipment to how eager the individual teachers and parents are to participate in a farm to school program. But once the programs are in place, adapted to the unique needs of the community, the benefits are clear. In studies, children eat an additional serving of fruits or vegetables per day when fresh, local produce is available in their school lunches, and school lunch participation increases by 3 to 16 percent.[16]

Food Policy Councils

Across America, food policy councils—which are groups devoted to changing laws to make a sustainable food system more achievable—are popping up at city, county and state levels. While a governor, mayor or legislative body will often create a council by legal means (i.e. issuing an executive order or passing a bill), concerned citizens can independently come together to form a council without the help of a government body.

Food policy councils are able to draw government departments out of their individual silos and facilitate their working together. For example, if one department's mission is to help local farmers market their products, and another department buys food, a FPC can work with both of them to initiate a program in which the government buys from local farmers. An FPC can also solicit community input to help government officials whose decisions affect the food system. If a state health department wants to set food safety standards but none of the health regulators understand farming, the FPC can bring the health regulators together with local farmers.

The groups and concepts I have written about in this chapter are in no way meant to be a comprehensive list of all the food-related organizations and ideas that are currently operating in the United States, nor are they an adequate representation of the different varieties of food-related activism that is happening concurrently. As the many vibrant communities of farmers, gardeners, eaters and activists across this country illustrate, the solution to the problems in our food system are not a mystery. For the most part, we know what to do, and in many cases, we're already doing it. Now we need to focus on implementing the solutions that work, like farm to school programs and community gardens, in a more universal way so that we can influence a larger percentage of the food eaten—and those who eat it.

6. BARRIERS TO BUILDING A SUSTAINABLE FOOD SYSTEM

If you believe that one person can make a difference by eating food grown locally by small farmers, imagine what the impact would be if restaurants, cafeterias, hospitals, prisons, airplanes—in short, any place that served food—began providing locally grown food. In this new eating world, instead of having to bring your own food to work in order to eat sustainably, local options would be available to you everywhere, from the office cafeteria to the delicatessen next door.

Unfortunately, getting local food into mainstream food establishments is a complex matter, made even more difficult by the practices of many chain restaurants. A study conducted in Colorado in 2003 found that nearly half of that state's independently-owned restaurants and institutions served local food, compared to only 11 percent of chains.[1] The restaurants in the study that bought food locally cited several factors for their decision, including face-to-face interactions with local growers and the ability to obtain fresher food. (One restaurant owner even said that an incentive for buying local was so that the farmer who grew his food could come and eat at his restaurant.)

Unlike the independently-owned restaurants, many of the chain restaurants cited in the study had less control over their purchasing decisions. This is a pattern consistent with national chains, as in many cases, corporate headquarters makes the purchasing decisions for individual restaurants in a chain, preventing people at the local level from actually buying locally. Corporate food chains also often use a competitive bidding process when purchasing food that tends to freeze out local growers.

Beyond the lack of control over purchasing decisions, several other roadblocks can stand in the way of a restaurant or institution buying locally. For example, think about a restaurant that buys its food from a single supplier. This restaurant doesn't have to deal with several different farmers, and no matter what it needs, it's always just a phone call away. However, a restaurant that buys locally often does not have that luxury. As an example, in my hometown of San Diego, a restaurant that wanted to buy locally would need to get its food from several different sources— Divine Madman for coffee, Café Moto for tea, Stone Brewery for beer, Jackie's Jams for jam, the Temecula Olive Oil Company for olive oil and balsamic vinegar, Bella Vado for avocado oil, Mama Ceseña's for tortillas, etc. The owner or chef could literally spend their entire day on the phone ordering ingredients, leaving little time for them to actually cook the food. (Recall the frenzied lives of Andrew and Robin Schiff from Spread, selecting their food from local farms by day, then hurrying back to the restaurant to cook that food at night).

Then there is the problem of reliability, as outside circumstances can often affect the ability of small farms to deliver their products. For example, even the best farmer had no power over the wildfires that swept the area outside of San Diego in 2007. One farm I spoke with told me they lost several acres of citrus in the fires, and I heard anecdotally about other farms that suffered even greater losses. When you run your own farm, disaster can strike anywhere, anytime. Wetherby Cranberry Farm, which I wrote about in chapter three, once lost three quarters of its crop to hailstorms, and a few farms I regularly bought from when I lived in Wisconsin have suffered significant damage from flooding. Even without natural catastrophes, the farm life can be unpredictable, as normal variations in weather can make a crop ripen sooner or later than planned, or cause other unexpected problems. Even wild animals can affect a farm's yield. When I visited Sage Mountain Farm in Aguanga, California, the farmer, Phil Noble, told me that coyotes were eating most of his watermelon. While a restaurant interesting in buying locally can cope with such uncertainty by buying from several farms so that they are covered if one farm experiences problems, many just find it easier to buy from a single food supplier.

Institutions and restaurants seeking to buy local, or even non-local, food from small producers can also bump up against the problem of product availability. Imagine a farmer with a small flock of chickens trying to provide enough eggs for an entire school district, or a Midwestern berry farm trying to supply berries to a restaurant that wanted to serve them year round. When you are dealing with a single, large supplier like Sysco, however, you never have any doubt that they will deliver what you ask for, when you ask for it, and in the quantity you desire. If they can't get you asparagus grown in America, they will get it from Chile. The truth is that small farms often cannot meet the quantity needs of large buyers, and even a large local farm cannot sell fresh fruits and vegetables out of season.

Despite the difficulties with getting local food into the mainstream food system, farmers are an innovative bunch, and as demand for local food grows, they will certainly continue to find ways to work around some of these barriers in order to sell their food to restaurants, schools and other institutions. And there is a demand for their products, as many of the respondents in the Colorado study said that they were interesting in buying locally, but ironically had never been approached by local growers. Quotes like, "I would buy locally if someone would come in and show me what they've got," and "We would buy locally if we were presented with a good quality product, at a good price," show that opportunities for direct marketing by local farmers to restaurants exist as long as one party is willing to approach the other.[2]

Barriers to Sustainable Food in Our Schools

In addition to the barriers that are simply facts of life (like the inability to grow food out of season), those seeking to bring local food into large, mainstream institutions often face many other obstacles as well, particularly when it comes to getting local food into our nation's schools. For example, while the city of Seattle has been at the forefront of the local food movement, it has been difficult to translate that forward thinking into the city's ability to feed its school children food that has been grown locally. Andrew Stout, owner of Full Circle Farm in Carnation, Washington, says that there is a great disconnect between the desire to see children eat sustainably and our "broken food system that cafeterias have co-opted for delivering a certain amount of calories for very little money."[3]

Money is in fact at the very root of the problem. In Seattle, a school has between $2.20 and $2.70 to spend per meal on each child.[4] After spending 4 percent of that money on equipment and supplies and 59 percent for labor, the most schools can spend on actual food is about $1.00. That typical dollar lunch translates into a 45 cent entrée served with 10 to 15 cents in vegetables, 10 cents worth of fruit, 10 to 20 cents of bread and/or dessert, with 22 cents of milk to wash it all down. By my estimation, this can buy half a local carrot or half a local beet as the vegetable, and a slice of local cantaloupe for the fruit. Perhaps by buying in bulk, a school could even afford a whole carrot for each student.

While the Seattle school district will buy locally grown and organic items when they are available and comparable in price, because of the immense scale of their food operation—they serve approximately 19,000 lunches per day—discussions about buying directly from local farms have never gotten very far. "I've actually scared a lot of farmers when I say, 'On this day I want this, but I need a gazillion pounds of it, and, oh, I can't pay you $5, I can pay you 25 cents,'" said Wendy Weyer, the district's dietitian and quality control supervisor.[5]

Serving local, pasture-raised meat is also often out of the question since the federal government gives schools free commodities as a subsidy to farmers, and no local farmer can beat a price of free. *Mother Jones* reported in 2003 that the government buys $800 million in farm products per year, which in turn constitutes 20 percent of the food served by our nation's schools.[6] Unfortunately for the health of our children, much of that free food is high in saturated fat; in 2001, the USDA purchased $350 million of beef and cheese, more than double the $161 million it spent on fruits and vegetables, most of which were frozen or canned. That ratio not only turns the food pyramid on its head, but it also favors the food industries (beef and dairy) that are responsible for nearly half of the greenhouse gas emissions in this country that are caused by food production and distribution.[7] However, there is one positive aspect to the acceptance of all these free commodities: it often leaves schools with more money to purchase local, farm-fresh food.

If the current system is not successful in getting local food into our schools, what about some of the sustainable solutions we have talked about, such as farm to school? Not surprisingly, there are problems there too. A well-named 2007 *New York Times* article ("Local Carrots with a Side of Red Tape") elucidated some of the difficulties that those trying to implement a farm to school program can face.[8] Richard Ball, who owns a farm in upstate New York, worked with the New York City school system for two years trying to figure out a way to sell them the carrots he grew on his farm. The school system had introduced local apples in 2005, resulting in a 400 percent increase in apple consumption by New York City's public school children, and was therefore eager to do the same with locally-grown carrots. However, because many schools lacked the ability to peel, cut and cook fresh carrots, the city needed the carrots they purchased to be in a form as easy to handle as the bagged baby carrots they were already serving. School districts trying to survive on tight budgets often cut back by removing their kitchens or building new schools without kitchens, replacing them with closet-sized food "rewarming" centers, essentially giant microwaves.[9] The most obvious solution was for local New York farmers to grow the variety of carrots that were used to make baby carrots, which are actually whittled down full size carrots, for the schools. One farmer took the risk, but the experiment was a flop; while the carrot variety for baby carrots grew well in a state like California, they did not take in the colder environment of upstate New York.

In the end, Ball and the New York school system decided to compromise and serve carrots cut in a coin shape with a crinkle cut, naming them Carrot Crunchers. The carrots were then tested at several schools, and the kids loved them. The next steps included drafting an agreement that allowed the substitution of carrots from other states during the times of the year when local farmers were unable to supply them, and setting a price that was no greater than what the school system currently paid for carrots. In the meantime, the processor who cuts the carrots into the coin shape has to send them to Vermont or Michigan for processing until he feels confident that his business from the schools can justify his investing in his own equipment.

Taken as a whole, many of the obstacles to introducing local food into our schools come down to a lack of financial resources. For the most part, our schools are strapped for cash, and if they need to rip out their kitchens and accept free commodities in order to be able to purchase textbooks or avoid laying off teachers, they will do so. Few would disagree with these priorities, but the question we must ask is why our schools are so hard up for cash in the first place? Do we not value the health of our future generations enough to fully fund our schools? Problems with school funding are even more troubling when you consider that the geographic areas where students are most at risk for obesity and diet-related chronic illness are also the least able to raise money from property taxes or charge students higher prices for lunch. Just as rich families can afford to eat organic at home while poor families struggle to even afford fresh fruits and vegetables, schools in more affluent areas that wish to improve their lunch programs or purchase food from local farmers are usually more able to do so than schools in poorer areas.

Barriers On the Farm

While small farms tend to excel at growing crops and raising livestock, they often face significant difficulties when it comes to the processing and selling of their products. Several groups have performed assessments attempting to ascertain the reasons small farms have trouble connecting with institutional customers and restaurants, and these assessments found that farmers, among other things, often lack sufficient packing and storage facilities, packing materials, liability insurance, as well as the proper means for transporting their food.[10] In addition, many farmers do not have sufficient knowledge of institutional markets or an understanding of the business cultures of produce distributors and food service managers. In a few cases, farmers were unable to sell to restaurants because they had already sold all their produce to their CSA customers or at farmers' markets.

However, the greatest obstacles that small farmers face in getting their products into the mainstream food system are often the result of burdensome government regulation. One of the more common pieces of feedback I received while researching this section of the book was that farmers frequently lack access to processing facilities, for everything from making jam from fruit to slaughtering animals. On first glance, this may not seem connected to government regulation—until you delve deeper into the issue.

Take jam, for instance. For San Diego-area farmers with excess fruit they are unable to sell, a woman named Jackie Anderson will purchase their fruit in order to make jams that she will then sell at markets, stores and local restaurants. Jackie notes that since it is difficult for farmers to simultaneously farm and make jam, she is thrilled to be able to fill that void for them. By filling this niche, Jackie is able to support herself with her jam business while local farmers have a solution for the ripe fruit they cannot sell.

Making jam requires more than ripe fruit, canning equipment, and good recipes, however; if you want to actually sell your jam, you need to make it in a commercial kitchen. Unfortunately, the government sets specifications for commercial kitchens and other processing facilities which are often unnecessarily elaborate and expensive for small businesses. In *Animal, Vegetable, Miracle*, Barbara Kingsolver writes about the extensive requirements for facilities that process milk:

> "Most states' dairy codes read like an obsessive compulsive's to-do list: the milking-house must have incandescent fixtures of 100 watts or more capacity located near but not directly above any bulk milk tank; it must have employee dressing rooms and a separate, permanently installed hand-washing facility (even if a house with a bathroom is ten steps away) with hot and cold water supplied through a mix valve; all milk must be pasteurized in a separate facility (not a household kitchen) with its own entrance and separate, paved driveway; processing must take place daily; every batch must be tested for hormones (even if it's your cow, and you gave it no hormones) by an approved laboratory. [11]

Kingsolver concludes that all of the strict rules around processing "might gratify industry lobbyists, by eliminating competition from family producers."

Kingsolver is correct when she explains how regulations can act as a means to eliminate competition from small producers. However, the problems she describes are not limited to just milk or jam. When it comes to processing meat, for example, state and federal laws often hinder a family farm's ability to do business. In 2008, an article appeared in *Edible San Diego* describing what happened when a local restaurant called The Linkery tried to add locally raised goat meat to its menu.[12] The Linkery bought its goat meat from a farm called RC Livestock, located in Fallbrook, California, a suburb of San Diego. The goats that were raised at RC Livestock were processed in Los Angeles, approximately 100 miles away. The proximity of the processing facilities to the farm was important not only for convenience and cost, but also to ensure the most humane possible treatment of the animals, who were raised on pasture and therefore unaccustomed to confinement or travel. When I spoke to Aley Kent of Heifer International, an organization dedicated to relieving global hunger and poverty by providing livestock, plants and education in sustainable agriculture to financially-disadvantaged families, she pointed out that many small meat producers are concerned about the stress their animals suffer while traveling to distant processing facilities.[13] Her words triggered memories of my own cats' distress when I moved from Wisconsin to California. During the long car ride, one of my cats, Meg, when she wasn't peeing in my lap, spent hours cowering under the driver's seat. If farm animals are anything like my cats, then providing them with a humane end to their lives involves more than just the act of slaughter itself.

Unfortunately, the meat processor in Los Angeles closed in early 2008, leaving Southern California without any USDA-inspected facility that catered to small producers. Aley told me that this is a common problem small producers face, as they are permitted by law to do small-scale processing on their farms—up to 1,000 chickens or 250 turkeys, for example—but cannot go any further without government inspection and licensing. She then referred me to Jim Hayes, a New York farmer who raises lamb, beef, chickens, turkeys and hogs. Jim built a processing facility on his farm and obtained a 5A license, which allows him to process up to 20,000 birds per year and to cut red meat under state inspection.[14] While he still must take his animals to a federally inspected plant for slaughter, by bringing the animals back to the farm for all remaining processing, he feels he gets a higher yield per animal and is more confident in guaranteeing to his customers that the meat he sells them comes from the animals he raised. However, under his 5A license, he still may not sell his meat wholesale, and he may only sell retail within the state of New York.

The dilemma that RC Livestock and The Linkery currently find themselves in— they cannot find a USDA inspected facility closer than six hours away willing to work with an independent organization—is not unusual. Aley explained to me that processing plants are often unwilling to deal with small producers because they prefer customers who will bring them a steady supply of animals. In addition, farmers must also consider the distinction between state-inspected and USDA-inspected processing facilities. Until 2008, state-inspected meat could not be sold across state lines under any circumstances, and even with a recent change in the law, it can only be sold under certain circumstances—a major barrier to farmers in states that lack a USDA inspected processing facility.

Food Safety Barriers—Good for Big Business, Deadly for Small Farmers

You wouldn't think that laws dedicated to improving food safety could be bad for small, sustainable farms? After all, one of the many benefits of buying your food from a small farm is the knowledge that that food is safe to eat, so any law that enhances food safety should automatically be good for sustainable agriculture? Unfortunately, the answer to that question is often no, especially when the government passes laws that are supposed to regulate enormous factory farms and other huge agribusinesses that have food safety or environmental problems, but which instead wind up negatively impacting small producers who don't even have food safety or environmental problems in the first place.

A perfect example of this is the "voluntary" but creeping-towards-mandatory National Animal ID System. It is hard to decide who NAIS benefits more—the RFID ear tag industry or factory farms—but it certainly does not help small farmers or their consumers. In fact, NAIS was in reality implemented to appease free traders who wanted to make American meat acceptable to international export markets—regardless of whether or not the program actually brings us any closer to food safety.[15]

While NAIS registers farms and animals so that the government can quickly track a sick animal back to its source in order to protect against "the devastation of a foreign animal disease outbreak," a small farmer, who raises animals on his or her farm from birth until death and only sells to a small group of customers in his or her community, will have no trouble tracking any sick animals.[16] In addition, because mad cow disease, or bovine spongiform encephalopathy (BSE), can be transmitted through food, if one cow contracts the disease, all the cows that eat the same food are at a higher risk of carrying the disease. If a cow were to test positive for mad cow, as three American cows have at the time of this writing, then of course our government needs to know where that cow came from to make sure other infected cows do not get into the food supply. And, in an enormous industrial operation, tracking where one cow came from would be difficult without having a system in place. However, in the case of the small, sustainable farmer, the need to track mad cow among his or her cows is highly unlikely, as in order to contract mad cow through food, a cow (naturally an herbivore) would have to eat another contaminated animal, and what sustainable farmer would feed a cow anything but grass, hay and perhaps grain? While the government-stated benefit of NAIS is consumer safety, I fail to see how crushing sustainable producers, whose products are also often the safest on the market, enhances safety. Tracking factory farmed animals may have its uses, but I believe a more effective way to enforce safety would be to close the many loopholes that lead to poor food safety in the first place.

Furthermore, NAIS places small producers at an extreme disadvantage to factory farms because while they must register each animal individually, a factory farm can register its animals (who, in the words of the USDA, "are raised and move through the production chain as one group"[17]) by lot. As a result, NAIS stands to harm many small producers due to the financial and time costs involved in complying with the program. One small farmer estimated the cost of implementing NAIS on her farm as $10,000, or 10 percent of her gross annual receipts.[18]

Finally, many small farms would rather go out of business than withstand the intrusive government oversight that complying with NAIS entails. Since small farmers frequently live on the land they farm, oversight of their animals winds up being oversight of them as well. For example, if a horse owner had to report each time their horse left the farm for a competition, he or she would in essence be reporting his or her own location and travel plans to the government. This issue is not so offensive to enormous factory farms, as government intrusion will not impact the personal lives of those who own and work the farm.

Financial Barriers

Broadly speaking, there is little opposition to the major goals of the sustainable food movement. Certainly, within individual communities, developers will sometimes covet the land used by a community garden, and occasional squabbles will arise due to the traffic or parking problems caused by a farmers' market. However, these disputes are usually minor and can be resolved fairly simply. In truth, one of the major obstacles the sustainable food movement faces is not opposition to its goals, but rather the money to achieve those goals. Invariably, whether via school funding (as we have seen), grants, or private philanthropy, growing the movement—any movement—requires money. And while the government gladly hands over our tax dollars to factory farms under the Environmental Quality Incentives program which it calls a "conservation" program, the sustainable agriculture movement has to fight for every penny it gets.

For example, during the debate over the 2008 farm bill, a long and arduous campaign by the Community Food Security Coalition and its allies resulted in keeping funding for Community Food Projects *the same as it had been before.* The program, which funds projects aimed at improving community food security, would certainly have benefited from increased funding, but with an unfriendly Agriculture Committee Chairman in the House (Minnesota Democrat Collin Peterson), the Coalition had to fight just to keep the status quo. And, at the same time that that battle was being "won," another battle was clearly lost when the USDA's Risk Management Agency's Community Outreach Partnership's budget was slashed in the Farm Bill from $8.3 million to $2.25 million. While many of these government grant programs sound arcane, they in fact result in real, tangible gains for sustainable agriculture and community food security. (The loss of funds from the RMA's budget didn't particularly concern me until I found out that a friend's very important food activism work was being funded by it.)

Market Barriers

One of the most significant barriers to the sustainable food movement, and one that is often hard to fight against because it goes contrary to the way people in this country are raised to think, is the unremitting belief that the "free market" can solve all our problems. While I don't want to get bogged down in the debate between market fundamentalism and the need for government regulation, the view that the market will take care of the excesses of corporations while at the same time keeping unhealthy food off our grocery store shelves has proven more times than not to be misguided. Unfortunately, this misguided belief in the free market is often a major impediment to the goals of the sustainable agricultural movement, as it pushes the view that government regulation is not needed, or that consumer pressure alone can force corporations can to regulate themselves.

An argument that is often made by those who oppose official regulation is that companies have the ability to "self-regulate" their own behavior. In this scenario, corporations can successfully police themselves, without the need for governmental interference. As an example of this, you may see a company like Kraft or PepsiCo advertise "better-for-you" foods to children as part of the fight against childhood obesity.[19] While this type of advertising will usually result in excellent PR for the company ("self-regulation" always make headlines and garner high praise from the media), its impact on public health is doubtful. In her book *Appetite for Profit*, public health advocate Michele Simon faults self-regulation because the rules that companies set for themselves are usually designed more to generate positive public relations spin than to actually provide solutions—"yielding benefits in the public/governmental perception arenas," as a 2008 article from Media Post, a website geared toward advertising professionals, put it.[20] In addition, Simon points out that even the most airtight self-regulatory claim lacks any sort of enforcement mechanism, as a corporation will never be punished if it violates its own voluntary rules.

Another claim made by those who oppose government regulation is that consumer-driven campaigns are able by themselves to alter the behavior of corporations. Perhaps the best example of one such campaign was the fight against recombinant bovine growth hormone. The hormone, popularly known by its acronym rbGH, makes cows more susceptible to painful diseases like acidosis and mastitis, thus leading to increased antibiotic use and higher "somatic cell count" (better known as pus) in the milk they produce. The hormone also increases the amount of a second hormone, IGF-1, in cows and their milk. Whereas the human body does not respond to bovine growth hormone, it does react to IGF-1 because humans produce an identical hormone. The effects of IGF-1 on humans have been linked to "twinning", giving birth to twins, and cancers of the breast, prostate and colon.[21] While the U.S. government legalized the use of rbGH in 1994, by 2009, consumer pressure had driven Wal-Mart, Starbucks, Kroger, Dannon, and countless other companies to stop accepting milk from cows that had been treated with rbGH for use in all or some of their products.

Is the consumer-driven campaign against rbGH proof that the free market works and that government regulation isn't needed? The answer is no. While rbGH is cruel to dairy cows and potentially harmful to human health, it was in much of our nonorganic milk for over a decade, and continues to be used today by 42.7 percent of large dairies, which comprise 15.2 percent of dairies overall, which translates to 17.2 percent of cows in the United States.[22] And though many companies no longer accept any milk from cows treated with rbGH from their suppliers, many still do. If governmental regulation is supposed to ensure that products are proven safe before they enter the food supply, then rbGH should never have been made legal in the first place.

That said, I think we must be careful about which regulations we pursue. The United States has no shortage of regulations that make no sense whatsoever, even if they were originally passed into law with good intentions. My call for more regulation is not by any means a call for more stupid regulation. We must not be shortsighted by calling for policies that help the environment while putting environmentally-friendly farmers out of business, or that help food safety while hurting restaurants that serve healthy food.

We must also remain cognizant of the political realities we face as we attempt to push a sustainable food agenda. For example, while we often debate whether to call for labeling or an outright ban of an undesirable food or ingredient, labeling requirements often spur companies to change their products for the better, for fear of putting negative information about the product on its label, making an outright ban unnecessary. In the case of trans-fat, food manufacturers are so eager to label their foods "0g Trans-Fat" that many are removing trans-fat from their products without the need for a national ban. Furthermore, labeling initiatives often meet with popular support as they are seen as providing increased freedom of choice for consumers, whereas calls for bans or other measures that prevent consumers from making choices, even unhealthy choices, often meet with stiff opposition, despite their positive intentions.[23]

Activist Barriers

In December 2007, the U.S. government announced that fruits, vegetables and whole grains would be added to the list of foods covered under the Women, Infants and Children program. For those who are unfamiliar with WIC, the program provides food, nutrition information and healthcare referrals to "low-income pregnant, postpartum and breastfeeding women, and infants and children up to age 5 who are at nutrition risk."[24] Currently, WIC provides food vouchers to over 8 million women and children each month.

The first comprehensive reform to the program since 1980, the addition of fruits and vegetables to the list of foods available to WIC recipients was designed to "address current nutrient inadequacies and excesses; discrepancies between dietary intake and dietary guidance; and current and future health-related problems in WIC's target population."[25] WIC has also run a Farmers' Market Nutrition Program since 1992, whose dual goals are to provide "fresh, nutritious, unprepared, locally grown fruits and vegetables to WIC participants, and to expand the awareness, use of and sales at farmers' markets." [26]

While the changes to the WIC program may sound like a boon to advocates of sustainable agriculture, the devil is in the details, as WIC provides only $6 to children, $8 to women and $10 to breastfeeding women per month for the purchase of fresh fruits and vegetables. [27] (My fruit and vegetable budget exceeds that per week!) When I brought this up with a fellow food activist, his disappointed reaction was, "What good is $6 of fruit per month?" At the same, I have spoken to WIC counselors who, having encountered participants in the program who report eating only one fruit or vegetable in an entire week and who also often mistakenly assume that fruit-flavored foods like Gummi bears count as fruit, think that the changes in WIC, though far from perfect, are an important step in the right direction.

This disagreement reflects the two approaches I have often encountered among those trying to reform our food system. On one side, there is the "glass half empty" crowd, who tend to get discouraged in the face of incremental gains and slow change. These people want the system reformed yesterday! On the other side are the "glass half full" camp who understand that $6 a month of fruit isn't a dramatic and final solution to the problem of childhood malnutrition and will gladly take whatever gains they can get today, then pick themselves back up tomorrow and continue the fight for change.

When working to make our food system more sustainable, it is important to keep in mind that both points of view have their merits, and to be careful not to allow the different approaches to put up artificial barriers within the sustainable activist community. While we continue to grow the sustainable food movement one farmers' market and one community garden at a time, we need to stay focused on our shared goals, and not allow differing beliefs on how to reach those goals to prevent us from coming together as a cohesive movement. As Benjamin Franklin once said, "We must hang together, gentlemen [and ladies]...else, we shall most assuredly hang separately."

The Greatest Barrier

Issues aside, in the end, the greatest barrier to truly growing the sustainable food movement is the government's refusal to recognize sustainable agriculture as superior to the conventional food system. You wouldn't think this would be such a strong barrier, but in many ways it is. For evidence of the challenges sustainable food advocates face, look no further than House Agriculture Committee Chairman Collin Peterson, who was once quoted calling consumers who pay extra for local or organic foods "dumb."[28] While the government will on occasion recognize the value of sustainable food and agriculture, for the most part it bows down to conventional, industrialized agriculture as the mainstream norm. Unfortunately, the best interests of the American people have not factored into many of the food-related decisions made by our government over the past few decades—decisions that were made by both major political parties. Without official acknowledgment that sustainable food and agriculture are vital to our survival—whereas industrialized food and agriculture jeopardize our very existence on this planet—our ability to transform government policies so that they establish a food system that nourishes our people and our land will remain limited.

That said, we now have an executive branch that came to power with grassroots support, and it has already demonstrated that it will side with the will of the people when they make their voices heard. For example, when nearly 90,000 people signed a petition calling for an advocate of sustainable agriculture to be appointed to a top position at the USDA, the Obama administration met with leaders of the petition drive and responded by appointing one of the requested choices, Kathleen Merrigan, to the number two post at the USDA.[29] In the end, government needs to be a large part of the solution to our food crisis, but it can only be so if we make it act in the best interests of the people. I believe that lack of popular outcry is why corporations have come to rule our food system, and with our urging, the government can work with us to take that system back.

The following chapters detail the platform I am proposing to reform our food system—my "Recipe for America." I have no doubt that some of my suggestions will be out of date within a few months of this book's publication, and I look forward to the day that my ideas are obsolete because that would mean that our food system is healthy and vibrant and reforms are thus unnecessary. More likely, however, are new outrages that will continue to make daily news headlines. (The week I am writing this brought news of farmers feeding cattle reject M&M's and potato chips as a means of coping with high corn and soy prices.)[30] I invite you to take these ideas as an overall blueprint to work from and to use the website RecipeForAmerica.org and my blog LaVidaLocavore.org to stay up to date on current issues and to celebrate our victories as we achieve them.

7. LABELING

A 2005 study of Americans' perceptions of their food system found that a majority support government policies that empower consumers to make healthier eating choices, with 61 percent of those surveyed supporting a law requiring restaurants to list the calorie count and fat content of all items listed on their menus, a number that rose to 70 percent when the law was specifically aimed at fast food restaurants.[1] In comparison, only 23 percent of survey participants supported a law setting a legal limit on portion size in restaurants. To most Americans, labels mean freedom of choice, and, if nothing else, we Americans love our freedom. For those of us in the sustainable agriculture movement, advocating for increased labeling on the food we purchase in grocery stores and eat in restaurants presents an excellent opportunity to make significant progress in an area where we have the support of a majority of the American people.

Labeling issues fall into three major categories: requiring restaurant menus to list nutritional information; requiring packaged food labels to alert consumers to specific details that food companies don't want them to know about; and regulating misleading labeling information.

A New Item on the Menu: Nutrition Information

2008 was a good year for proponents of menu labeling. In May, after several years of legal challenges by the restaurant industry, menu labeling was finally passed in New York City, requiring all restaurants with fifteen or more locations nationwide to display calorie counts on their menus.[2] Later in the year, Multnomah County, Oregon (which includes the city of Portland) and King County, Washington (Seattle) joined New York in requiring restaurants with fifteen or more locations nationally to list calorie counts.[3] King County also stipulated that restaurants were not subject to the new rules unless they had over $1 million in gross annual revenues and standardized menus and recipes.[4] California also joined the labeling movement, passing the first statewide menu labeling law, which will be phased in over the next three years.[5] And, late in the year, the city of Philadelphia passed what has been called the most stringent menu labeling law in the country, as in addition to forcing establishments that have fifteen or more locations nationally to list nutrition information, restaurants in the city of brotherly love will also be required to list levels of saturated and trans fat, sodium and carbohydrates on all printed menus.[6]

Since the packaged products available in our grocery stores have long listed nutrition information, it may seem odd that restaurants have not fallen under the same guidelines. A quick look back at the history of food labeling, however, shows why restaurants have, for the most part, escaped labeling laws.

Beginning in the 1970s, fast food restaurants, particularly large chains like McDonalds, began resisting attempts to label their products, often countering suggestions to provide nutrition information where consumers might actually read it (i.e. on product packaging or on menu boards) with their own preferred solution—wall mounted posters and brochures, usually printed in tiny fonts.[7] Restaurants and their front groups have continued this tactic to the present day, for example, proposing pamphlets with the nutrition information located on the back, in a tiny font of course, as a counter to California's efforts to require menu labeling.[8]

In 1986, under threat of a lawsuit, McDonalds finally started providing in-store nutrition brochures (then hurried to tell the press about it before the government had announced the settlement, applauding themselves for *voluntarily* providing nutrition information). Fast-forward to today, and McDonald's is now fighting *for* labels on packaging, the very thing they had so vehemently opposed in the past. The reason for this seeming change of heart is that McDonald's favors the labeling option, which gives consumers nutrition data *post-purchase*, to having calorie information posted on menu boards—a measure that might make someone think twice before ordering a 1,160 calorie 32 ounce triple thick chocolate shake.[9]

While the public climate is currently in favor of increased labeling, food activists on the front line of this battle will not emerge victorious unless they continue to remain vigilant, as the restaurant industry is not going to back down easily. As an example of how aggressive, even deceitful, they can be, before New York City succeeded in passing its menu labeling law, the New York State Restaurant Association paid a physician, Dr. David Allison, to write a document showing the impact the proposed law would have on consumers. Allison, of course supported the NYSRA's opposition to the law, arguing that there was no evidence consumers would eat less with menu labeling, but that, on the contrary, they might actually eat more when they saw calorie counts posted on menus.[10] (Because of the clear conflict of interest he engaged in by writing this document, Allison was forced to resign as President of the Obesity Society before even taking office.[11]) Now that New York's labeling law is in effect, researchers will be able to finally gather valid, impartial data that can show whether or not menu labels in fact influence consumer food choices, and if so, how.

Furthermore, during the battle over labeling in California, pro-restaurant industry advocates proposed an alternate labeling law which would have allowed restaurants to choose from a number of different labeling options, including brochures or posters.[12] The arguments of the restaurant industry in this case were an attempt to make the public health advocates who were calling for menu labeling look inflexible, as the industry groups claimed that restaurants were not opposed to providing nutrition information, but were simply offering customers freedom of choice. No doubt the restaurant lobby will play the same game in other states and on the national level as more and more municipalities pass labeling laws.

And, if they cannot take down labeling initiatives through the legislative process, the restaurant industry will attack through the legal system, as to date, lawsuits have been filed in both New York and San Francisco in an effort to overturn labeling laws in each city. (In February 2009, the 2nd U.S. Circuit Court of Appeals upheld the New York City menu regulations in the face of a challenge by the New York State Restaurant Association.)[13]

While we will need to support our elected representatives when they are brave enough to take on the restaurant industry, and push them with frequent phone calls and letters when they are not, success is well within our reach when it comes to menu labeling.

What the Labels Won't Tell You

Unlike the food served in restaurants, the packaged products available in supermarkets have long offered us a wealth of nutrition information. However, in many cases, what is important is not what it says on the label, but what it doesn't. For example, does the food you are about to eat contain Genetically Modified Organisms (GMOs)? Was rbGH used on the cows that produced the milk you are about to drink? Are the sugars listed in the glass of juice you are going to give to your children natural or added? Packaged food labels currently do not list any of this information.

Let us address each of these issues so you can see why their absence on packaged food labels is a potential public health problem.

GMOs

As of 2008, 92 percent of soybeans, 86 percent of cotton and 80 percent of the corn grown in the United States was genetically modified to either resist weed-killing chemicals or to assist the plants in producing their own insecticides.[14] Despite these staggering numbers, few of us are aware that we are eating genetically-altered food. According to a poll taken in 2006, only one quarter of Americans believed they had eaten GMOs, when in reality nearly 100 percent of us have eaten GM food since its introduction in 1996.[15] (The same poll found that only 34 percent believed that GM foods were safe to eat.) Unfortunately, Americans get very little say about GMOs because manufacturers in this country are not legally required to label their GM food, the way they are in Europe, Japan and Australia. When asked, however, Americans overwhelmingly support the labeling of GMO's: a 2008 CBS News poll found that 87 percent supported the labeling of food that contained GM ingredients.[16]

After attending BIO 2008, an international biotechnology convention, I have come to my own conclusions about GMOs. What struck me most while attending the convention was that most GM food proponents aren't bad people—in fact, they genuinely believe they are helping the world by reducing the amount of pesticides used on our crops and by creating drought-resistant plants. Unfortunately, they do not back up their often worthy aims by trying to come up with alternatives to GMOs, then weighing whether those alternatives are better for our environment and our food system than GMOs. To them, it is GMOs or nothing. However, if they took the time to ask a farmer, particularly one well-versed in sustainable methods, how to help plants cope with drought conditions, they would hear a variety of recommendations on how to improve soil quality. In fact, the pros of such an approach over genetic modification are many: soil is available immediately and can be used on all plants (not just the varieties that Monsanto or Syngenta has engineered to withstand drought); soil does not require government approval or regulation; no one will sue you for saving your seeds; the methods for improving soil are time tested; and good soil will bring additional benefits to your plants, whereas a seed engineered to withstand drought may not also be engineered to withstand pests and disease or to produce in great quantities. While companies like Monsanto—and their supporters—start with the assumption that GMOs are the answer, to date, I have not seen a use for GMOs that cannot be accomplished naturally.

This discussion, however, is a tangent. While weighing the pros and cons of GMOs is relevant when debating whether or not the government should allow GM food and in what circumstances, when it comes to labeling, the question should not be whether or not GMOs are the solution to the world food crisis or harmful to our health, but simply: Do we have a right to know what is in our food? I believe the answer is yes, and, according to polls, so do most Americans.

Would You Like Some rBGH in Your Coffee?

If we have the right to know what types of chemicals and other unnatural ingredients are in the food we eat, then don't we have also have the right to know how that food was produced? For example, shouldn't you be able to find out if the milk you just put in your morning cup of coffee came from cows that were injected with recombinant bovine growth hormone (rBGH)? Unfortunately, Monsanto, the company that invented rBGH, has worked diligently over the years to try and keep that information from consumers.

Soon after rBGH went on the market in the United States in 1994, Monsanto sued two dairies, one in Illinois and one in Texas, for marketing their milk as rBGH-free; ultimately, both dairies agreed to modify their labels. This aggressive stance would become typical of Monsanto's strategy against its often smaller competitors. "If history's any indicator, Monsanto likes to pick on smaller guys," said Joseph Mendelson, legal director of the nonprofit Center for Food Safety.[17] Nearly a decade after the Texas and Illinois lawsuits, Monsanto went after another dairy over its rbGH-free labeling, targeting Oakhurst Dairy in Maine, who at the time labeled its products with the claim, "Our Farmers' Pledge: No Artificial Growth Hormones." "We state what we are trying to do, simply and honestly," said Stan Bennett, owner of the Portland-based dairy. "It's my right—and obligation—to inform [customers] of the facts."[18] Monsanto asserted that since the FDA had already approved rBGH, and because milk from both treated and untreated cows is "the same," that allowing labels like the one Oakhurst put on its milk was unfair because it might make consumers question the safety of rBGH. In the end, under pressure from Monsanto, Oakhurst Dairy agreed to add a qualifying statement to its milk labels, separate from the farmers' pledge and in smaller type, reading, "FDA states: No significant difference in milk from cows treated with artificial growth hormone."[19]

In 2007, rBGH labeling came under further attack when Pennsylvania Secretary of Agriculture Dennis Wolff issued a law banning rbGH-free labels in the Keystone State, making Pennsylvania the first of many states, including Indiana, Kansas, Missouri, New Jersey, New York, Ohio and Utah, to consider restrictions on rBGH-free labels. In protest, a coalition of groups ranging from Physicians for Social Responsibility to Ben and Jerry's came together to fight the Pennsylvania ban. Backed by statistics that showed that 80 percent of Americans wanted to know if rBGH was used on the cows that produced their milk, the coalition was able to convince Pennsylvania Governor Ed Rendell to reverse the labeling ban in early 2008.[20] Despite the victory for rBGH-free labeling in Pennsylvania (and subsequently, Indiana, Kansas, Missouri, New Jersey and Utah), the labeling debate continues to rage on in several state capitals.[21] Ultimately, the best solution would be a national law granting dairies throughout the country the right to label their milk as coming from cows free of rBGH.

A new twist in the rBGH tale came in August 2008, when Monsanto sold off its rBGH business to Elanco, a division of Eli Lilly.[22] At the time of this writing, no one knows if Elanco will be as aggressive in pursuing labeling bans as Monsanto was, nor if it will be as proactive in funding studies that come to positive conclusions about rBGH (for example, a study published in 2008 that claimed there was no significant difference among milk with conventional, rBGH-free and organic labels).[23] However, Rick North, Project Director of the Campaign for Safe Food, doesn't expect Elanco to deviate much from the aggressive practices established by Monsanto. "They will insist that there are no human or animal health risks, in spite of the scientific evidence," he writes. "They will continue to keep tight-lipped about sales figures. And they have already put out incorrect statements, such as rBGH is "'genetically identical to what cows produce naturally.'"[24]

Added Sugars

When you eat a piece of fresh fruit or drink a glass of milk, your first thought wouldn't be that you just consumed something filled with sugar. However, both milk and fresh fruit do in fact contain sugar—except that the sugars contained in those foods are *naturally* occurring in the foods themselves (fructose in fruit and lactose in milk). And when you eat foods that contain natural sugars, your body receives nutrients along with the sugar, which is conducive to good health.

On the other hand, if you drink a can of soda, or eat a cookie you baked at home, the sugar in both of those were *added* during the preparation process—from high fructose corn syrup in the soda to the cup and a half of sugar you added to the cookie dough. Unlike foods with predominantly natural sugars, foods and beverages that contain high amounts of added sugars are most likely low in nutrients. Therefore, when you eat a diet high in added sugars, instead of consuming food that is healthy for your body, you are "displacing foods that provide nutrients that reduce the risk of osteoporosis, cancer, heart disease, stroke, and other health problems" such as obesity.[25]

Unfortunately, too many Americans enjoy diets that are high in added sugars. According to the USDA, we consume approximately 97 pounds of added sugars per year—that's 28.7 teaspoons of added sugars per day, or 460 "empty" calories that supply us with no additional nutrients.[26] If you look at how we are filling our bodies with all these added sugars, you will find that almost half the time we are drinking them: 33 percent of added sugars come from soft drinks, 10 percent from fruit drinks and 3 percent from tea. Other sources are baked goods, dairy desserts, candy and breakfast cereal.[27] Basically, we are eating (and drinking) sugar, fat, sodium, preservatives, and artificial coloring and flavoring, while we are not eating fiber, vitamins, minerals and phytochemicals.

Currently, while the amount of *total* sugars is listed on a food label, there is no way for consumers to tell whether a food's total sugars are naturally occurring or added, as they are not listed separately. Take a cup of blueberry yogurt, for example. The label on the container will tell you the ingredients and the amount of total sugars, fat and calories. While milk and blueberries each naturally contain sugar, many food producers add additional sweeteners to their products. So, if you are looking for the brand of yogurt with the least amount of added sugar, you would have no way of knowing which one to pick based on the label alone.

In 1999, the Center for Science in the Public Interest (CSPI) petitioned the FDA to require that labels reveal how much added sugar food contains. In addition, CSPI also asked the FDA to establish a maximum Daily Reference Value of 40 grams (10 teaspoons) of added sugars, representing 10 percent of a 2,000 calorie per day diet. The CSPI did not pick that number out of thin air; it is a worldwide standard, recognized by the WHO's Global Strategy on Diet, Physical Activity, and Health, and implicitly recommended by the USDA's Food Pyramid. However, the FDA, as it had with CSPI's previous petitions in 1986 and 1993, denied the 1999 petition. Among the reasons the FDA has given over the years for denying CSPI petitions is lack of public interest in reducing the consumption of added sugars, lack of conclusive evidence that sugar is associated with chronic disease conditions and the inability to distinguish between added sugars and naturally occurring ones.[28]

I agree with CSPI that labeling added sugars is a necessary step in helping Americans make healthy food choices. Furthermore, if added sugars were labeled, the FDA would then be better able to regulate other claims that are made on food packages (i.e. "Low in sugar" or "Reduced sugar"). Education via labels is one of the most non-invasive steps we can take in the battle against the public health problems posed by added sugars in our food.

COOL

Because of the wide discrepancy in laws governing food preparation and processing from country to country, an important labeling issue is what is known as "country of origin labeling," or COOL. Country of origin labeling lets customers know where their food came from, so they can avoid food imported from countries that have poor health records, or which do not engage in proper oversight of their food systems.

COOL was first passed in the 2002 farm bill; however, its implementation was delayed, with the exception of seafood, until September 2008, when the USDA published a "final rule" outlining the law's specific measures.[29] However, as the rule was drafted by the notoriously lax Bush Administration, its provisions were often defined as loosely as possible, and featured numerous loopholes. For example, the rule requires labeling for "muscle cuts and ground beef (including veal), lamb, pork, chicken, and goat meat; wild and farm-raised fish and shellfish, perishable agricultural commodities; peanuts; pecans; ginseng; and macadamia nuts." However, because of a narrow definition of what kind of retailers are included in the rule, food sold at restaurants, cafeterias, bars, butcher shops and fish markets are exempt. In addition, the rule included a very liberal definition of processing, which had the effect of exempting many processed foods.* This means that while frozen peas have to be labeled, a bag of frozen peas and carrots is exempt. Raw peanuts must be labeled, but roasted peanuts are exempt. Pork chops must be labeled, but bacon is exempt. And so on.

Currently, advocacy groups such as the Consumers Union are calling on the USDA to close the loopholes in the COOL rule by narrowing the definition of processed foods and by requiring butcher shops and fish markets to label their products.[30] While Agriculture Secretary Tom Vilsack has written that he has "legitimate concerns" about the Final Rule "promulgated by the previous Administration," for now, he is only requiring that industry voluntarily comply with stricter COOL standards.[31]

Misleading Labels

So far in this chapter, we have discussed what it means for our health when there are no labels on our food (in the case of res-

---

*The final rule defined processing as "cooking (e.g., frying, broiling, grilling, boiling, steaming, baking, roasting), curing (e.g., salt curing, sugar curing, drying), smoking (cold or hot), and restructuring (e.g., emulsifying and extruding)" or adding ingredients other than water, salt or sugar.

taurants) or when the labels provide us with too little information. However, sometimes the problem is not a lack of information, but rather information that is misleading. Take, for example, Urban Detox, one of the Function brand of beverages. On its label, Urban Detox says that it will "Help fight hangovers and rid your lungs and sinuses of airborne pollutants using the 'smog-scrubbing' anti-oxidant N-acetyl cysteine (NAC) and natural anti-inflammatory prickly pear extract." While the label also includes the FDA disclaimer, "This product is not intended to diagnos, treat, cure, or prevent any disease," most people picking up a bottle of Urban Detox would likely assume that the drink will cure them of their hangovers while at the same time detoxifying their lungs and sinuses.

Products like Urban Detox fall into the category of what are called "nutraceuticals"—foods that claim to provide beneficial health effects. Dr. Stephen DeFelice coined the word in 1989 by combining "Nutrition" and "Pharmaceutical," and while the term is commonly used in product marketing, it in fact has no regulatory definition.[32] In effect, nutraceuticals blur the line between food, dietary supplements and drugs. The preponderance of nutraceuticals on the market bring up an important labeling question: How can we help consumers obtain the information they need about the health effects of what they eat and drink without allowing food manufacturers to make misleading claims about their products?

To understand how we reached the point where a company like Function can (presumably) legally claim that one of its beverages banishes hangovers, it is helpful to look briefly at the FDA's long and ultimately fruitless efforts to regulate dietary supplements. Over the past century, whenever the FDA has tried to forbid unsubstantiated label claims in order to keep harmful products off the market, it has been strongly opposed by the dietary supplement industry, and, ironically, more than a few consumers. According to author and food expert Marion Nestle, "the preponderance of available evidence suggests that if they were tested, the great majority of supplements now on the market would prove to be no more effective than placebos and that a few would be demonstrably harmful."[33]

Food became intertwined with the supplement fight in 1984 when Kellogg's placed a label on its All-Bran Cereal that read, "The National Cancer Institute believes eating the right foods may reduce your risk of cancer. Here are their recommendations: Eat high fiber foods. A growing body of evidence says high fiber foods are important to good health. That's why a healthy diet includes high fiber foods like bran cereals."[34] Opening wide the anti-regulatory door that the All-Bran "health" claim (which Kellogg's declared at the time was not a health claim at all, but simply a message from the National Cancer Institute that the company was "simply printing,")[35] had pushed ajar, the Nutrition Labeling and Education Act of 1990 permitted the FDA to allow health claims to be listed on foods and dietary supplements so long as these claims could be backed up by "significant scientific agreement" among "qualified experts."[36] The NLEA allowed labels to claim, for example, that dietary soluble fiber from whole oats reduced the risk of coronary heart disease.[37]

Four years later, the myth of even token regulation was shattered with passage of the Dietary Supplement Health and Education Act of 1994, which expanded allowable claims to include "structure/function" statements (statements proclaiming how ingredients might alleviate a nutritional deficiency, improve the structure or function of a part of the human body . . . or promote general well-being.")[38] As Nestle writes, the result was that "the supplement industry won the right to state that an untested product promotes healthful cholesterol levels, but not that it lowers cholesterol; that it supports regularity, but not that it relieves constipation; that it maintains healthy joints, but not that it reduces symptoms of arthritis."[39]

The final nail in the FDA's regulatory coffin on health claims on labels came in the 1999 court case Pearson v. Shalala, when the D.C. Court of Appeals ruled on appeal that denying a health claim that lacked "significant scientific support" was illegal on First Amendment grounds.[40] The decision created legal and empirical hurdles to the FDA's efforts to reject petitions filed in support of health claims for dietary supplements.[41] When I asked lawyer and food policy expert Ellen Fried what should be done about regulating health claims on labels, her answer was simply, "Turn back the clock to before Pearson v. Shalala." I agree with Fried's stance, as I don't want to grant Nabisco the right to claim that Oreos cure cancer, or give Kraft the ability to state that eating a box of Mac 'n Cheese every day will prevent AIDS. Of course, neither of these companies has ever made such ridiculous claims, but since we already have a line of beverages claiming to banish hangovers and detoxify lungs and sinuses, who knows what some bright marketing department is going to think up to put on our food labels next.

8. FOOD SAFETY

The U.S. government currently handles food safety with the same level of competence that FEMA demonstrated trying to help the victims of Hurricane Katrina. Food scares seem to happen one after the other, forcing consumers to keep constantly evolving lists of the foods they need to avoid. One day its spinach; the next day, ground beef, or tomatoes, or jalapeños, or sprouts, or pet food or peanut butter. In 2008, the FDA spent an embarrassing six weeks trying to locate the source of a salmonella outbreak, first telling consumers to avoid tomatoes before finally discovering that the actual cause of the outbreak was peppers.[1] As with labeling, it should not be difficult to garner the support of the public and even many legislators in calling for a safer food system, as wanting to know that our food is safe to eat is not exactly a controversial point of view.

However, controversy is injected into discussions of food safety when we begin to consider how to achieve the goal of safe food. Sometimes, government policies that may appear effective lack true regulatory bite because they were designed not to ruffle the feathers of big business. Other times, a policy may be good for safety, but cause the food in question to become less nutritious because of a change in ingredients or growing practices. Yet another flaw in food safety policies is designing laws that hurt small, sustainable producers by forcing them to yield to requirements that are expensive to implement (think of the National Animal ID System). Our goal as citizens should be to advocate for strategies that ensure a safe food supply while simultaneously maintaining a level playing field so that sustainable food producers can compete in the marketplace.

Food Safety Laws Sometimes Hurt More Than They Help

Too often, it seems as if the food safety policies in this country were put together with the idea that our food is grown in sterile laboratory conditions. For example, following several E. coli outbreaks in 2007, California implemented the "Leafy Greens Marketing Agreement" in an attempt to prevent the future contamination of leafy greens. Among other things, the agreement discouraged the development of microbial life in the soil, despite evidence that sustainable methods which encourage the growth of soil microbes reduce harmful pathogens like E. coli 0157:H7. The agreement also encouraged farmers to destroy hedgerows and other non-crop vegetation around their fields—though natural vegetation around farm fields provides a habitat for birds and beneficial insects that prey on pest species, thus reducing dependence on pesticides.[2] The truth is that when you do things correctly, you can have biodiversity without compromising food safety.

There are, of course, legitimate circumstances where it is necessary to keep other forms of life away from our food, like when a farmer covers his ripening blackberries with nets to keep out scavenging birds. And it also makes sense that a farmer should not make cider from apples that fell on the ground where they may have come into contact with animal feces. On the whole, though, we need to keep in mind that safety methods suitable for laboratories and hospitals are not necessarily the ones that should be put in place for the food we eat.

Another thorny issue in food safety is traceability, i.e. being able to trace food back to its source. On one hand, we need to have a strong traceability system in place so that food recalls, when they are necessary, can be done quickly and accurately. In the summer of 2008, when Whole Foods recalled beef tainted with E. coli, it discovered that the beef, which it had obtained from Coleman Natural Foods, had in fact been processed at Nebraska Beef, a meatpacker with a history of food safety violations.[3] As this illustrates, when corporate dynamics are so complex with mergers, outsourcing and licensing so that it's nearly impossible to tell where our food originally came from, it can create potentially deadly health problems. While increasing traceability in our food system is important for this reason, at the same time, it should not take the place of practices that will prevent food safety problems from occurring in the first place. (I cannot imagine any law the government can pass that would establish stronger food safety than a farmer eating his own food, or better traceability than a consumer buying directly from a farmer.)

Lastly, if every safety measure in place happens to fail, the government should have the right to require a food recall. However, at the present time, the government can do no more than recommend a recall. During the 2007 pet food recalls, for example, the FDA knew of companies that had (or possibly had) sold tainted pet food, but refused to disclose their names before those companies voluntarily issued their own recalls.[4] Even if a company ultimately complies with the FDA's recommendation for recalling food, timing matters when tainted food is already on grocery store shelves and people are eating it every day. How many unnecessary food-borne illnesses have Americans been exposed to because the government lacked the authority to mandate a recall? The food safety bills currently in Congress, if passed, will give the FDA the authority to mandate a recall.[5]

Microbial Contamination

To best illustrate how to prevent food-borne illnesses, it is helpful to use an analogy that every person reading this book (above a certain age) should be well-acquainted with: practicing safe sex. While food-borne illnesses are typically not transmitted from animal to animal, or from animal to human, via intercourse, the process of preventing them can easily be compared to the process of preventing STDs.

For the sake of simplicity, I will focus on E. coli, even though it is certainly not the only bacteria that can cause illness in humans. E. coli is a bacteria common to the digestive tract of many animals—including humans. Normally, E. coli serves a useful function in the body by suppressing the growth of harmful bacterial species as well as synthesizing large amounts of vitamins. However, one strain of the bacteria called E. coli serotype O157:H7 produces toxins in humans that can cause severe diarrhea and in certain cases, acute kidney failure.[6] Because it lives in the digestive tract, the way a person usually contracts E. coli O157:H7 is by ingesting the fecal matter of animals. Exposures that can result in illness include "consumption of contaminated food, consumption of unpasteurized (raw) milk, consumption of water that has not been disinfected, contact with cattle, or contact with the feces of infected people."[7]

To begin the safe sex analogy, think about a farmer who owns several cows. The cows graze out in the pasture, and whenever they defecate on the ground, the dung beetles immediately take care of the manure. If this farmer has no plans to ever eat her cows, this would be the food safety version of abstinence. However, very few people practice abstinence, and no one can abstain from eating food.

If one day the farmer decided to butcher one of her cows and eat the meat, because the cow ate only grass and came into contact with little manure from other animals, the farmer would most likely not get sick by eating meat from the cow. And even if she did get ill, she would know where the cow came from and could easily prevent the illness from spreading by disposing of the remaining meat. This is like practicing monogamy. However, most people sleep with more than one partner during their lives, and few people have access to the food safety equivalent of monogamy—local pasture-raised meat.

But, if during the course of our lives we sleep with multiple partners, our risk for contracting an STD increases. Similarly, a cow's risk for contracting E. coli goes up when it lives in crowded pens with other animals, travels with other animals in rail cars and when its meat is mixed with the meat of other animals to make ground beef. (Would this be the food safety equivalent of taking a different person home every night from a bar?)

We all know that the best way to practice safe sex is to wear a condom. And, because condoms sometimes break, if you are truly practicing safe sex, you should go to the doctor for routine testing, especially if you have had unprotected intercourse. The same principles should also apply to food safety: reduce high risk activities as much as possible, but also test to make sure that the precautions you took were effective.

However, the solution favored by industry is irradiation. In other words, nuke the food until the microbes are dead and it no longer matters if there's "shit in the meat."[8] As Carole Tucker Foreman, an Assistant Secretary of Agriculture in the Carter Administration put it, "Sterilized poop is still poop."[9] While technology has many benefits, I would rather see us figure out a real solution to our food safety problems, preferably one that wasn't literally so full of shit.

Reducing Risk

Short of engaging in the food versions of abstinence and monogamy, what can we do to reduce the risk of farm animals becoming infected with microbes that make humans sick while also reducing the risk of those microbes getting into our food? In the case of E. coli, we simply have to keep feces out of our food supply—which should be a goal whether or not E. coli is in the picture.

When cows and hogs live on factory farms, their manure is collected in lagoons. Occasionally, these lagoons are drained and the manure spread on fields as fertilizer. Often, the manure is not composted, which would heat it to a high enough temperature to kill off any microbes that are present. Therefore, it would make sense to require factory farms to compost their manure before using it as fertilizer. Using dung beetles is another option for disposing of small amounts of manure, but since the beetles are sensitive to antibiotics, they would not be useful on factory farms where large amounts of antibiotics are in use. One way to specifically reduce the risk of E. coli O157:H7 is by changing cows' feed from grain to grass or hay a few days before slaughter, as grass-fed cows generate less than 1 percent as much E. coli O157:H7 in their feces as grain-fed cows.

Many large factory farms also produce more waste than they can properly dispose of. Because humans also poop and very few of us compost our own waste, society has developed sewage treatment plants. Sending factory farm manure to sewage treatment plants would undoubtedly be more expensive for factory farm owners, but part of the cost of raising livestock should be the cost of properly disposing of their waste.

For hogs in particular, the Swedish "hoophouse" method, which we discussed in chapter two, is another possible solution. The advantages of hoophouses are many: the cost of building one is one third that of a confinement facility, they are energy efficient, require no mechanical ventilation and allow pigs to engage in their natural social behaviors.[10] In addition, hogs raised in hoophouses require fewer antibiotics in comparison to confined hogs, and their mortality rate is lower as well. As for the manure—recall the example of Gary Onan, whose hoophouse hog operation made $14,000 from composted manure whereas a neighbor with a confinement operation spent $10,000 to have his liquid manure drained from a lagoon and spread on a field.

Once cows reach the slaughterhouse, the greatest risk factor for E. coli is the speed of the production line. As Eric Schlosser wrote in *Fast Food Nation*, "stomachs and intestines are still pulled out of the cattle by hand; if the job is not performed carefully, the contents of the digestive system may spill everywhere."[11] Schlosser adds that a single worker may gut 60 cattle per hour, with the hourly spillage rate, depending on the skill of the worker, running as high as 20 percent. If workers become less accurate when the production line moves at a high speed, then the solution is obvious: slow down the production line. Unfortunately, to the best of my knowledge, none of the food safety bills currently before Congress address either line speed or unhealthy factory farm conditions.

Increasing Testing and Inspection

While the adoption of one or more of these food safety ideas would reduce the amount of E. coli and other pathogens in our food, to be really confident that what we are eating is safe, processors should be required to perform microbial testing. One of the best examples of an effective microbial testing program was put in place after an E. coli outbreak caused by the fast food chain Jack in the Box in 1993. Following the outbreak, the company hired David M. Theno, a food scientist, who implemented a program requiring each company that manufactured hamburger patties for Jack in the Box to perform microbial testing on their beef every fifteen minutes during processing.[12] Why can't our government require a similar system in which food processors (particularly of foods that have been the cause of previous outbreaks, like ground beef) are required to perform microbial testing at regular intervals and maintain records of these tests? This could also apply to farmers who grow produce (particularly leafy greens, which have been the cause of several E. coli outbreaks) as well, since they should be required test the water they use for irrigation and processing for a range of pathogens. Alternatively or in addition, USDA or FDA inspectors could perform microbial tests either routinely or during random inspections.

In 2009, the USDA finally announced plans to test ground beef at packing plants up to four times per month, depending on the volume of ground beef a plant produces.[13] While this is certainly better than having no testing at all, it pales in comparison with the Jack in the Boxes requirement that packing plants test ground beef four times an hour.

Antibiotic Resistance

Another danger to food safety comes from the antibiotic resistance that develops in agricultural animals because of the enormous amount of non-therapeutic antibiotics (antibiotics given to animals when they aren't sick) that are administered to them. By one estimate, three-quarters of the 25 million pounds of antibiotics used each year in animal agriculture are given for non-therapeutic purposes (compared to only 3 million pounds of antibiotics ingested by humans annually for medical purposes).[14] These antibiotics, which are used to promote growth, kill most bacteria but allow a small amount of antibiotic-resistant bacteria to survive and breed. If any of these bacteria cause illness in humans, the antibiotics the bugs are resistant to will be ineffective. Unfortunately, about half of the antibiotics used in agriculture belong to classes of drugs that are also used in human medicine. Because antibiotic resistance to a particular drug can lead to resistance to other drugs in the same class, we must keep classes of drugs used for humans out of the agricultural system.[15] The World Health Organization attributes "infection that would not have otherwise occurred, increased frequency of treatment failures (in some cases death) and increased severity of infections" to "non-human usage of antimicrobials."[16]

In order to keep antibiotics effective for human medicine, the European Union banned antibiotic use in animals for growth promotion in 2006. Representative Louise Slaughter (D-NY) and Senator Ted Kennedy (D-MA) introduced a bill to do the same (Preservation of Antibiotics for Medical Treatment Act) in the United States House of Representatives and Senate, respectively, but to date the United States has not passed the bill, or any other similar bill that would accomplish the same goals. As a matter of fact, when Rep. Slaughter introduced her bill in the House, the National Pork Producers Council shot back that the bill would be "detrimental to the health and wellbeing of pigs, would increase production costs and the price consumers pay for pork, and could jeopardize public health."[17] Above all, we need to put human health above the profitability of a few corporations by implementing a ban on non-therapeutic antibiotic use in animals, as the EU has already done.

Mad Cow Disease

Known officially as bovine spongiform encephalopathy, or BSE, "mad cow disease" falls within a class of illnesses known as transmissible spongiform encephalopathies (TSEs). In addition to cows, many other species can suffer from TSEs, including humans, sheep and mink. TSEs can also cross species barriers, as a human eating BSE-infected material from a cow can contract the human form of the disease, known as variant Creutzfeldt-Jákob Disease, or vCJD. The symptoms of vCJD include clumsiness, fatigue, and diminishing eyesight, eventually progressing to blindness, paralysis, and ultimately, death. vCJD is similar to CJD, Creutzfeldt-Jakob Disease, a human TSE that existed before the version linked to BSE was identified. Under normal circumstances, CJD shows up in humans at a rate of about 1 per every million.[18]

While there are numerous theories that try to explain the rare and seemingly spontaneous appearances of TSEs, we do know how TSEs spread after they show up in a specific population. The British mad cow epidemic of the mid-1990s, for example, occurred because cows, which are naturally herbivores, were fed the remains of other infected cows. When humans consumed the cows, the disease was able to cross the species barrier, infecting the humans with vCJD (although at a much lower rate than the number of cows infected with BSE). Fortunately, preventing epidemics of TSEs is easy: simply keep animals infected with TSEs out of the human and animal food supply.

The practice of feeding cows to other cows was not limited to the UK, but was also common in the United States. So, is the practice illegal now? The answer is: sort of. In 1997, the FDA banned the feeding of ruminants (cows, sheep and goats) and mink to other ruminants.[19] As an exception, calves may be fed cow blood instead of milk. But pigs and chickens could still eat cows, and cows could still eat pigs and chickens. In addition, the law continued to allow the feeding of cows to cows at low levels. In 2008, the FDA issued a final rule expanding the 1997 law, which stated that cows over the age of thirty months had to be inspected before they could be consumed by humans and if they don't pass, they aren't permitted in the animal food chain either.[20] Also, according to the new rule, the most high-risk body parts for TSE—the brains and spinal cord—of cows over thirty months are not allowed in animal feed under any circumstances, though cattle under thirty months of age are still allowed in animal feed. Since TSEs require a long time to develop, it was believed that cattle under thirty months were at a lower risk of spreading TSEs. However, Michael Hanson of the Consumers Union pointed out when this rule was first proposed in 2005 that 10 percent of Japan's known cases of BSE were in cows under the age of thirty months.[21] Hanson therefore advocates that the United States follow the UK in prohibiting the feeding of any mammal material to agricultural animals.

In addition to following Hanson's recommendations, we must also test cows for BSE because, unless we test every single animal, we are unlikely to discover every case of BSE that occurs. Testing every cow is possible (Japan does it), but as of the summer of 2008, the U.S. tested only 0.1 percent of its cows for BSE.

(The Consumers Union advocates testing every cow over the age of twenty months.)[22] Furthermore, the USDA must also permit private mad cow testing, a practice it currently bans. In August 2008, the U.S. Court of Appeals upheld the USDA's right to prohibit Creekston Farms Premium Beef LLC from testing every one of its animals for mad cow by declining to sell Creekston the necessary test kits.[23] If we are going to truly halt the spread of mad cow disease, then companies that wish to continue doing business with other nations that require more stringent testing than the U.S. currently performs, as well as those who want to sell their products to consumers in this country, must be allowed to test their animals without the government actively preventing them from doing so.

Mercury in Fish

While mad cow disease is a product of lax regulation in the meat industry, yet another food safety problem comes to us via our rivers, lakes and oceans, a result of the "bioaccumulation" of toxic substances. Bioaccumulation occurs when organisms at the bottom of the food chain ingest small amounts of a particular substance. As the lower species are eaten by animals higher up on the food chain, the toxins from the lower species accumulate within the bodies of the animals that have eaten them. Because of this, animals at the top of the food chain—particularly those with long life spans—are especially vulnerable to bioaccumulation. Keep in mind that humans are at the very top of the food chain.

Because it has a long shelf life and is an extremely popular food, much of the attention around bioaccumulation is focused on the problem of mercury in tuna. Where does this mercury come from? The main sources are emissions from coal-fired power plants and waste incinerators, which release mercury into the atmosphere. Whenever it rains, the mercury returns to the land, entering our waterways and oceans. While on average, tuna contains far less mercury than swordfish, shark, king mackerel and tilefish, most Americans do not eat the latter foods on a regular basis.[24] However, Americans love their tuna, consuming approximately 1 billion pounds of canned and pouched tuna per year, with canned tuna being the second most popular seafood product in the U.S. [25]

While the human body can rid itself of mercury, it does so at a slow rate that varies from person to person. A New Jersey woman named Deborah Landvik-Fellner experienced mercury poisoning due to her eating a can of albacore tuna daily over a twelve year period.[26] Eventually, her hair began falling out, her speech became slurred, her memory failed, her hands started to shake and she began to experience heart problems. After suffering these symptoms for five years and seeing numerous doctors, she was finally tested for mercury. The results were shocking—her blood contained ten times the level of mercury that the EPA considers safe.

While Landvik-Fellner experienced her symptoms after eating tuna over an extended period of time, for children and women of childbearing age, mercury poses dangers even at low levels. Because our bodies cannot excrete mercury quickly, a pregnant woman can carry enough mercury in her body to harm the fetus within her. According to the EPA, exposure to methylmercury (the kind of mercury found in fish and shellfish) in the womb can result in neurological impairment affecting "cognitive thinking, memory, attention, language, and fine motor and visual spatial skills." [27]

Despite the grave risks that mercury in fish presents, the government's current warnings, as well as its actions to prevent future mercury contamination, are extremely lacking. The EPA and FDA jointly advise women who may become pregnant, pregnant women, nursing mothers, and young children to eat only twelve ounces of fish weekly, of which only six ounces should be albacore tuna. It is recommended they avoid shark, swordfish, king mackerel and tilefish entirely.[28] However, a study by the Environmental Working Group found these recommendations insufficient, concluding that women of childbearing age, on top of not eating shark, swordfish, king mackerel and tilefish, should also avoid tuna steaks, sea bass, oysters from the Gulf Coast, marlin, halibut, pike, walleye, white croaker and largemouth bass. The EWG also recommended that women of childbearing age eat no more than one meal per month total of any of the following: canned tuna, mahi-mahi, blue mussel, Eastern oyster, cod, Pollock, salmon from the Great Lakes, blue crab from the Gulf of Mexico, white channel catfish, and white lakefish.[29] For more individualized advice, the EWG offers a "tuna calculator" on their website; when I entered my personal statistics, it told me I was allowed 4.4 ounces of albacore tuna per week, assuming that I ate no other fish.[30] If I had followed the government's advice, while I would think I was safe, I would actually be at risk of overdosing on mercury.

To adequately respond to the danger of mercury in fish, the government should immediately take three steps. First, it should revise its mercury warnings to reflect more accurate information. Whether it relies on the Environmental Working Group's study or performs a new study of its own, the government should update its recommendations to include all the species of fish that women of childbearing age should avoid, as well as offering revised recommendations for tuna consumption that do not put women at risk for harming their unborn children.

Second, the government should require that warnings be placed on the labels of tuna cans and packages. As we saw with the battle over nutrition information on restaurant menus, warnings do little good unless they are placed in locations where consumers are likely to see them. While the government has quietly advertised its currently insufficient tuna advisory via brochures in doctors' offices, the tuna industry has attempted to negate any effects of that advisory with its own $25 million pro-tuna advertising campaign.[31] Consumers have a right to understand the risks they face when they eat diets rich in tuna, and the most appropriate place for a warning is on tuna labels.

Finally, the government needs to curb, if not end, mercury pollution. At the tail end of the Clinton administration, the EPA made an effort to do so, ruling that coal-fired power plants violated the Clean Air Act and proposing a 90 percent reduction in mercury emissions by power plants by the year 2008. The Bush administration rolled this ruling back, however, instead calling for a 70 percent reduction in emissions by 2018. 2008 has now come and gone, and with a new president in office, we need to be as aggressive as possible in reducing mercury emissions. Also, the Obama administration should not allow for cap and trade, for unlike gasses that disperse evenly throughout the world regardless of where they were first emitted, mercury is a heavy metal which can create "hot spots" where high concentrations are found.

Chaos in Washington

The problems and issues discussed in this chapter merely skim the surface of food safety in America. (I haven't even touched on items like melamine contamination or trade with countries that have lower food safety standards than ours.) But even the limited information provided here should make it obvious that our government is not doing what it should be to keep our food supply safe. One of the reasons for the government's inaction is that we do not have a food safety system that was created in a logical, comprehensive manner. Currently, thirty-five separate laws govern our food safety regulations, and these laws are administrated by twelve agencies run by six cabinet-level departments.[32] There is also little apparent logic behind how these agencies divide up their food safety responsibilities. To quote Marion Nestle: "The USDA, for example, oversees production of hot dogs in pastry dough; the FDA regulates hot dogs in rolls. The USDA regulates corn dogs; the FDA regulates bagel dogs. The USDA regulates pepperoni pizza; the FDA regulates cheese pizza . . . The USDA regulates beef broth, but the FDA regulates chicken broth; for dehydrated broths, the agencies switch."[33]

Ironically, despite the massive bureaucracy that is responsible for food safety in this country, there are still large gaps in the system. For example, who is responsible for making sure our eggs are safe to eat? While The FDA inspects shell eggs, they do not inspect hen houses.[34] The Animal and Plant Health Inspection Service (APHIS) makes sure chickens aren't sick—but salmonella, a common problem in chickens, does not make chickens sick, so the APHIS doesn't monitor it. The Agricultural Marketing Services (AMS) grades eggs for size and quality, but does not check for safety. The Food Safety and Inspection Services (FSIS) inspect liquid, frozen, and powdered egg products—but not shell eggs.

Part of the reason our food safety system is such a mess is because it was designed piecemeal over the course of the last century, with no set of specific, guiding principles. It also does not help that the USDA has the dual purpose of promoting and regulating agriculture, and when these interests conflict, the promotion side usually wins out. And while the FDA, under the Department of Health and Human Services, is tasked with the clear purpose of keeping our food and drugs safe, because this role proves incompatible with large campaign contributions from pharmaceutical and agricultural companies, Congress keeps the FDA perennially underfunded.

In the wake of the salmonella peanut butter crisis of early 2009, a number of food safety bills were introduced in Congress. However, while members of both political parties agree that food safety reform is needed, legislators lack agreement—even within their own parties—on what should be done.[35] Some legislators, like Rosa DeLauro (D-CT), wish to see food safety fall under the auspices of the FDA because of the USDA's conflict of interest as promoter and regulator of agriculture. Others, like House Agriculture Chairman Collin Peterson, are advocating for the opposite solution, wishing to see the USDA gain full authority over food safety issues on the farm most likely for the same reasons that DeLauro and others wish to move food safety responsibility away from the USDA.[36] Without any agreement, it appears unlikely that any major reorganization of food safety agencies will occur in the near future.

9. PROTECTING CHILDREN

I have a confession to make. Back when I was in junior high school, I took the lunch money that my parents gave me each week, and instead of spending it on lunch like I was supposed to, I bought junk food. My favorite were Nutty Bars, peanut butter filled wafers dipped in chocolate. And I didn't even have to go to the candy store to obtain my sugar fix, as my school sold junk food directly to its students. Unfortunately, my school was not an anomaly—since the early 1970s, schools in the United States have been permitted to sell foods of "minimal nutritional value" (i.e. candies, cookies, soft drinks, etc.) if the proceeds from sales of such foods benefit the school or school-related groups.[1] While indulging in sweets may be a common rite of youthful passage, when our schools themselves sell junk food, it teaches kids that cookies and candy, instead of just being an occasional treat, are in fact acceptable to eat on a regular basis, often, as my own experience illustrates, in lieu of regular meals.

Since a majority of Americans view poor eating habits as a matter of individual choice, they have tended to oppose laws— for example, on portion size in restaurants—that limit people's right to choose what and how much they eat. However, many people who are for freedom of choice when it comes to regulating portion size are more than willing to accept government intervention when it specifically safeguards the health of our children. And because children spend a large part of their lives in public schools, the government does in fact have a direct role in monitoring what they are eating. Therefore, it is important to examine the major issues that affect children's eating habits, with an eye toward establishing a system that is beneficial to the short term health and long term food attitudes and behaviors of our youngest citizens.

Pouring Rights

During my junior year of high school, my school district signed a contract with Pepsi, which gave the company the exclusive right to sell its products on school premises. Known as pouring rights agreements, these types of contracts have become commonplace over the past decade. In the 1990s, soft drink manufacturers, having sold their products for years through vending machines on school and college campuses, decided to increase their marketing outreach to students. An important part of these efforts were the procurement of pouring rights, wherein soft drink companies pay for the exclusive right to sell their products in schools.[2] In addition to building "a stable school sales base," pouring rights agreements allow soft drink companies to continuously advertise their products through the display of company logos on school property, where they can be regularly viewed by students, including those too young to be reached by regular advertising.[3] In addition to their influence on young minds, pouring rights agreements also create financial incentives for schools to push soda, juice, fruit drink and sports drinks to their students, which in turn provide children with unnecessary empty calories—the last thing they need with childhood obesity on the rise.

Once a school district signs a pouring rights agreement, the schools within that district typically see an increase in the number of vending machines on their grounds, and individual schools that did not previously have vending machines now find themselves with them.[4] The end result is unsurprising: soft drink consumption increases among the students, which in turn earns the school district financial rewards from the soft drink company. Ultimately, our children are unknowingly paying for their education with both their pocket change—and their health. While a small majority of Americans oppose soda machines in schools (with or without pouring rights agreements), opposition increases when they learn about the financial incentives built into pouring rights agreements.[5]

Competitive Foods

The chips, cookies, fruit drinks, sodas, candy and other junk food—in short, any food that is not regulated as part of the USDA's school lunch program—that schools sell to their children are referred to as "competitive foods" because they compete with the traditional lunch program for children's money and appetites. On a federal level, the regulation of competitive foods has varied over the decades, but for the most part, the government has very little say over which competitive foods are sold in schools, and where and when children may purchase them. Currently, the only foods that the federal government does not allow to be sold in school cafeterias during lunchtime are so-called "foods of minimal nutritional value," which include soda water, "water ices" made with no fruit or fruit juice, chewing gum and certain candies (hard candy, cotton candy, jelly or gummy candy, licorice, marshmallow candy and candy-coated popcorn).[6] However, these foods are allowed to be sold outside the cafeteria at any time during the school day, as well as inside the cafeteria when it is not lunch time.

Unlike competitive foods, school meals are designed to establish lifelong healthy eating habits. Because these meals are prepared in compliance with federal Dietary Guidelines, "participants in school meal programs have been shown to consume better diets than nonparticipants."[7] When competitive foods enter the scene, however, participation in school lunch programs declines. During a 1994 hearing conducted by the Senate Agricultural Committee, Carol Meiki, a food service employee for the Chicago Public Schools, testified on how vending machines in Chicago-area schools competed with the school lunch program, noting that "one school's food sales dropped by $700 in the first week after soda machines were installed." Meiki said that it was difficult to get the machines removed because they generated revenue for the schools, and because the schools received gifts and cash incentives from the soft drink companies. She cited an example in which Coca-Cola distributed free 20 ounce soda bottles in a school lunch room as an advertising technique, testifying that participation in the school lunch program "dropped by half that particular day."[8]

Whenever the USDA has tried to set more stringent regulations on competitive foods, it has been prevented from doing so by court decisions. Therefore, stricter regulation needs to come from Congress. During a March 2009 congressional hearing, Dr. Katie Wilson, the Nutrition Director of the Onalaska Public Schools in Wisconsin asked that all foods sold anywhere within schools during any time of the day be regulated with the same set of rules. Senator Tom Harkin (D-IA) replied that he had tried to do so in the past, but had not been successful. While I hope that Harkin will succeed in achieving this goal sometime in the near future, as recently as 2008, he was unable to get a bill passed that would have strengthened the standards for foods of minimal nutritional value.[9] Also, with childhood obesity playing so prominently in the news, some food manufacturers, such as Mars, are eagerly committing to voluntary and often lax nutrition standards for foods sold in schools in an effort to prevent Congress from taking regulatory action. Such voluntary agreements allow companies to continue marketing to children in schools, thus building brand loyalty at a young age so that children will be more likely to purchase their products outside of school.[10] If members of Congress believe that the problems of unhealthy competitive foods can be remediated by voluntary actions alone, they may not move forward with regulatory reform.

School Funding

On top of needing money to educate our children, schools also need money to feed them—i.e. to build and maintain kitchens and employ lunchroom staff. And those lunchroom staffs require adequate time to prepare and serve food, while children need enough time to eat. (Lack of funding leads to both overcrowded schools and short lunch periods.) The cliché "there's no free lunch" is literal in this case. In addition, programs such as school gardens and farm to school, which are great ways to teach children about healthy eating while fostering an enjoyment of fresh fruits and vegetables, cannot exist unless they are funded. Even if we ignore special programs like school gardens and farm to school and focus on regular lunch programs, many schools still lack proper funding, particularly if they want to add nutritious items to their menus.

Connie Boldt, Food Service Director for the Knoxville Community Schools in Knoxville, Iowa, testified before Congress in March 2009 that offering healthier foods like whole grains and fresh fruits and vegetables resulted in increased costs for her lunch program.[11] Boldt, whose schools won a Gold award as part of the HealthierUS School Challenge, a USDA-sponsored program that tries to curb childhood obesity by encouraging schools to feed children nutritious, healthy food (schools can be certified Bronze, Silver, Gold or Gold of Distinction Schools based on how well they follow the program),[12] said that increased food costs "will make reapplying for the HealthierUS School Challenge more difficult in the future."[13]

Because of the lack of sufficient funding, schools are often forced to rely on pouring rights agreements and on the sale of competitive foods to pay for things that the government can't or won't subsidize. Ironically, if, under the current climate, we removed our schools' ability to profit from selling junk food, we would be leaving them even more strapped for cash than they already are. By failing to properly fund our schools today, we will be making a imprudent investment in our students tomorrow, as children who develop diet-related chronic illnesses will pay dearly as adults in terms of poor quality of life and lost wages, as well as overburdening our healthcare system. Thus, there can be no justification for allowing soft drink companies and junk food peddlers to determine our children's diets. Currently, under the Fresh Fruit and Vegetable Program, the federal government funds the distribution of fresh and dried fruits and fresh vegetables in a small number of schools in each one of the fifty states.[14] This program is a move in the right direction, but it is only a very small step towards where we need to be.

Advertising

Growing up in the 1980s, some of my earliest memories are of cereal commercials featuring memorable characters such as Cap'n Crunch and that silly rabbit that wanted his Trix. I also remember asking my mother to buy certain cereals because they had toys inside, and begging for a Happy Meal at McDonalds for the same reason. I even had my fifth birthday party at a McDonalds. While I came of age in a period when advertising toward children was on the rise, today's kids are bombarded in ways that I was never was as a child—for example, with things such as "advergaming," which are free video games on corporate websites that promote products and brands. The statistics tell the real story: in 2006, children between the ages of 2 and 17 were subjected to $1.6 billion in food advertising; of that amount, $492 million was spent on the marketing of soda, $294 million on fast food and $237 million on breakfast cereal.[15]

Imagine how you would feel as a parent if one of those advertisers showed up at your house and asked for a private meeting with your six-year old? Yet we allow the equivalent of that on TV, in stores, online and in our schools. While these advertisements are loosely "self-regulated" by the Children's Advertising Review Unit (CARU) of the Better Business Bureau, if you watch Nickelodeon or most other children's programming, you can clearly see that these self-regulations aren't very effective.

When called on their behavior, corporations usually offer solutions like voluntary moratoriums on specific advertising to children (i.e. not advertising the most offensive, unhealthy foods to the youngest age groups). But such voluntary arrangements typically serve only to get the media, activists and/or regulators off of the corporation's back, while leaving loopholes that allow them to continue their aggressive advertising campaigns. And even if a company promises not to advertise on shows where the target audience is children, they are still able to advertise during adult programs—like *American Idol*, for example—which reach a large number of children. My friend's four-year-old son, knowing that his mother hates junk food and commercialism and therefore values PBS for its lack of commercials, tauntingly pointed out to her one day that McDonalds was sponsoring a show he was watching on PBS. While the show was technically commercial-free, the golden arches were flashed across the screen all the same.

Regardless of who a product is being advertised to, it is ultimately the parent who purchases the food and thus has final say over what a child eats. As clear cut as that may sound, however, it ignores the "nag factor"—the nagging, whining and possibly screaming or crying scene a child influenced by advertising will make in the middle of the grocery store if he or she does not get the cereal or soda or candy they want. Corporations know that many parents who may not initially choose to buy a certain product for their child will be much more inclined to do so if buying it is the only way to get the kid out of the store without throwing a fit.

In 2008, the Federal Trade Commission recommended that entertainment companies license their characters only for use in advertisements for "healthier" foods and drinks. In addition, they also recommended that companies that market food and drinks to children intensify their educational campaigns to teach kids about healthy eating and exercise.[16] While these recommendations make it sound like the government is doing something to address the problem of advertising toward children, in reality, the proposals are completely voluntary, and thus legally unenforceable. They simply allow companies to continue their current advertising methods toward children, while conducting token "education" campaigns to try and appease their critics.

Whatever the solutions to limiting advertising to children wind up being, they will not be truly effective unless they are shaped by three basic principles:

- They must be mandatory, not voluntary.
- They must not allow normal marketing to continue unabated while the company conducts an ineffective "education" campaign.
- They must not permit the promotion of "healthy" foods by popular movie and TV characters.

Though they may seem ambitious in scope, these principles are in fact merely starting points. A true solution would end all marketing in schools, as well as banning any marketing that targets children under the age of eight, who do not understand that commercials are intended to persuade and therefore cannot distinguish between advertisements and program content.[17]

However, in order to get to that point, we will have to leap several hurdles, including defining what exactly we consider marketing. Is a Coca-Cola logo on a vending machine in a school marketing? What about corporate sponsorship of a school's sports team? How about General Mills' Boxtops for Education program, which encourages children to turn in boxtops from General Mills' cereals in exchange for financial donations to their schools? While the line between marketing that is dangerous to our children and marketing that is helpful can often become blurred in today's world, where corporate involvement is routinely accepted in most walks of life, we must strive to create laws that close the loopholes that give corporations undue influence over what our children eat. A good move in this direction was a bill that Representative Peter Koutoujian introduced in the Massachusetts state legislature in 2007 which would have "prohibit[ed] advertising and marketing of manufacturers' consumer goods and products on school grounds or on property that is owned or leased by a public school."[18] Unfortunately, the bill got bogged down in political battles and never became law. Ultimately, what we need is the political will to pass laws that are effective in regulating advertising that targets children.

One last—but vitally important—point that needs to be addressed during any discussion of corporate marketing to children is the role that parents play in the process. Shouldn't parents be responsible for the TV shows and movies their children watch, as well as which purchasing decisions are ultimately made in the household? The answer, of course, is yes—but it is a qualified yes. While a family can throw out their TV sets and home school their children in order to shield them from all forms of corporate marketing, why should they be forced into such extremes measures? Susan Linn, author of *Consuming Kids: The Hostile Takeover of Childhood*, writes that it is "naïve or disingenuous to believe that one family in isolation can combat a $17 billion industry working day and night to undermine parental authority, and to bypass parents and target children directly with messages that usually aren't good for them. Parents do have a responsibility to work to protect their children from the onslaught of advertising and marketing, but they can't do it alone."[19] Senator Tom Harkin chimes in with a similar statement, saying "No question, many parents need to make better choices for their children. They need to say no. But there are practical limits on what we can expect. It is just not realistic to think that most parents are going to deny their children access to TV on Saturday morning and after school. And, for goodness sake, why do we have a situation where conscientious parents have to protect their children from the ads on Saturday-morning TV?"[20]

In the final analysis, this discussion comes down to economics: advertisers would not spend billions of dollars on ads and marketing toward children if it did not work. While we cannot eliminate all forms of advertising, just as we cannot mandate healthy eating or ban junk food, at the very least we can take steps that will allow children to develop the cognitive ability to recognize marketing for what it is before they are confronted with it at such a high frequency.

Artificial Food Dyes

I have a friend named John who told me that when his stepson was very young, the boy suffered from behavioral problems consistent with Attention Deficit Hyperactivity Disorder (ADHD). While trying to find a solution to these problems, John and his wife came across the work of Benjamin Feingold, a pediatric allergist who back in the early 1970s proposed that artificial colors and artificial flavors cause hyperactivity in children. Putting Dr. Feingold's theories into practice, John and his wife started feeding the boy a diet free of artificial food additives. Within a few weeks, the boy's behavioral problems had vanished.

The experience of John's stepson is not unique. Between three and ten percent of school age children in America suffer from behavioral disorders such as hyperactivity or ADHD,[21] and numerous studies indicate that these children's conditions are exacerbated by eight artificial food dyes: Yellow 5, Red 40, Blue 1, Blue 2, Green 3, Orange B, Red 3, and Yellow 6.[22] Over the past fifty years, Americans' exposure to artificial food dyes has risen sharply, from 12 milligrams per capita per day in 1955 to 59 mg per capita per day in 2007.[23] These dyes are used in countless foods and candies, including Oscar Meyer's Lunchables, Starburst, Skittles, and M&Ms, and are also often used to simulate the color of fruits or vegetables. For example, the topping on McDonald's strawberry sundaes is colored red by food dye. While the United Kingdom has already begun phasing out these dyes in their food, they are still legal in this country.[24]

While food dyes adversely affect only a small percentage of the population, allowing them to remain legal makes life needlessly difficult for the children who are susceptible to their harmful effects. Even if parents like John and his wife are astute enough to discover the cause of their child's behavioral problems, they will still have a difficult time keeping these dyes out of their children's diets. Sadly, many parents never discover the cause of their children's problems, and instead give them medication or enroll them in special needs school programs. In the latter cases, taxpayers end up paying for food manufacturer's use of artificial food dyes.

If artificial food dyes can be removed from foods in the U.K., the only reason they must still be in use in this country is profitability. However, it makes no sense that corporations should be permitted to line their pockets by using substances that harm children. The eight food dyes named above should be phased out in the U.S. as soon as possible, and in the interim, products containing them should bear warning labels.

While this chapter tackles only a few of the many food-related health issues that confront our children these days, the ones discussed are some of the most important, as well as some of the easiest to fix. Certainly, the government cannot make up for parental irresponsibility, but it can make sure at the very least that our children are focused on learning and not on corporate marketing when they are in school. Doing so will not undermine a parent's right to allow their children to bring junk food to school, but it will ensure that children whose parents pack them healthy lunches will not toss them out in favor of cookies once they get to school.

Likewise, imposing a limit on advertising to children under the age of eight will help parents to teach their children about healthy eating without their messages being undermined by corporate advertising. While only a responsible parent can ensure that a child eats healthily, as citizens we can come together to make these parents' jobs a lot easier.

10. HUMAN AND ANIMAL RIGHTS

While as a society we collectively regret the stain that legalized slavery left on our nation's past, slavery, in fact, still exists in the United States today. Think about the last time you ate a tomato: could it have been picked by a slave? If you bought it at a store or a restaurant, it is quite probable. Though modern day slavery is, of course, an extreme (though not non-existent, as we shall see), what are the odds that the farm workers, who picked your tomato or your grapes or a number of other crops, were well-treated and fairly paid? Our food system is literally built on the exploitation of human beings, as well as animals. Unfortunately, while most of the abuses imposed on humans are technically illegal, the government turns enough of a blind eye to allow them to continue.

In May 2008, a 17-year-old undocumented Mexican immigrant named Maria Isabel Vasquez Jimenez set the kind of record you don't want to set—she became the youngest farm worker to die from heat exhaustion.[1] Her death was not only tragic; it was preventable. According to the law in California, where Maria worked harvesting grapes for West Coast Grape Farming, owned partly by Fred Franzia of California's Bronco Wine Company which produces the Charles Shaw brand of wine known popularly as "Two Buck Chuck,"[2] workers must be provided at least one quart of water per hour during their working shift, and those feeling the effects of the heat must have access to a shaded rest area for paid recovery periods of at least five minutes and as long as they need.[3]

On May 14, Maria began working at 6:00 in the morning, receiving only a single water break at 10:30.[4] At 3:40 p.m., in 95-degree heat, she collapsed. However, Merced Farm Labor, the farm labor contractor she worked for, delayed bringing her to a hospital. Instead, another employee first took her to a drugstore and tried to revive her with rubbing alcohol.[5] When Maria was finally taken to the hospital, she was in a coma with a body temperature of 108 degrees. She died two days later. After her death, the hospital informed her fiancé that she was two months pregnant with their child.

While California passed the most stringent heat law in the nation in 2005 after four farmworkers died while working in the field, the effect of the law seems to be negligible, as three farmworkers died in the state the following year, and in 2007, state labor inspectors found that more than half of the employers they audited were in violation of the law. In addition, Merced Farm Labor had been fined and cited in 2006 for failing to train its employees on heat safety, but, at the time of Maria's death, state labor inspectors hadn't visited the company since the violations had been recorded.[6] Perhaps the reason that the heat stress regulations have not prevented more deaths is that the average fine companies paid for farmworker deaths between 2005 and 2008 was $9,900 (excluding the $262,000 paid in the case of Maria Jimenez).[7]

Sadly, the farm-related death of Maria Jimenez was not surprising, as farm work is second only to mining in causing worker deaths, and second only to construction in causing disability.[8] Why are the lives of farmworkers seemingly worth so little to our society? The answer is simple: many farmworkers are undocumented immigrants. For example, of the approximately 700,000 farmworkers in California, half are undocumented immigrants, mostly from Mexico.[9] For many people, it is easier to direct anger at immigrants seeking work in our country than it is to try and change a system that allows their mistreatment.

And where is the government in all of this? For the most part, ignoring the problem. While farmworkers and their families have little ability to contact the government and advocate on their own behalf, the businesses that exploit them do have such access, creating a situation where the government, even if it wants to help, usually hears only one side of the story. Furthermore, consumers in America like cheap food, which is what cheap farm labor produces, so politicians are not routinely pressured to investigate the working conditions of farmworkers. Finally, a great majority of farmworkers don't speak English, or speak it as a second (or even third) language, so it is very difficult for them to communicate with the government, or with anyone other than their fellow farm workers for that matter.

It is only in extreme situations, such as the death of Maria Jimenez, or in cases of outright slavery, that the government becomes involved. In November 2007, three farmworkers in Immokalee, Florida escaped from a truck they had been locked in. A week later, police raided the house the men had been living in and found more than a dozen workers living in a truck, vans, and a wooden shed "hardly fit for goats."[10] The workers later told of the harrowing existence they were forced to endure, working for meager wages "while accruing charges for two meager meals a day, with extra charges tacked on for beer, soda, even water, until the debits outstrapped their wages."[11] And quitting wasn't an option, as those who tried to leave were hunted down, beaten and returned to captivity. Eventually, six people were indicted for "harboring illegal aliens," which hardly describes the enormity of the crimes they had committed.[12]

Why does our government wait for crimes of such a magnitude to occur before it intervenes? Don't all workers deserve a safe and healthy workplace, as well as fair wages? If anyone is worthy of our collective anger, it is the "illegal employers" who prey on undocumented workers just to help their financial bottom lines. Unfortunately, right now the practice of farmworker abuse is so widespread that I can only conclude that these "illegal employers" are engaging in such practices with relative impunity. Perhaps if the punishment incurred for violations of laws protecting workers were substantial—not a mere $9,900 fine—these employers would view upholding workers' rights as important?

Despite the fact that the harsh treatment of farmworkers in this country is for the most part ignored by government and the media, some groups have begun to organize to bring their message directly to the public. The Coalition of Immokalee Workers— whose workers were involved in the Immokalee slavery case— have been particularly successful in publicizing their cause. The CIW workers spend their winters in Florida harvesting tomatoes and citrus, moving up the east coast following the availability of work during the warmer months.[13] Although their name initially made me believe they were just a single group of farmworkers in one particular agricultural area, in fact these workers are responsible for harvesting nine out of ten tomatoes in America during the winter months.[14] Half of the workers are Mexican, while the rest are Guatemalan, Haitian and African-American. When they are able to find work, (which is not a guarantee on a day to day basis) the CIW workers are paid 40 to 45 cents for each 32 pound bucket of tomatoes they pick.[15] To make $50 in a day, a worker must pick two tons of tomatoes! Bypassing the government and even their employers, the CIW appealed directly to consumers to pressure major fast food and grocery chains into agreeing to pay an extra penny per pound for the tomatoes they purchased. An additional penny a pound increases the workers' pay to 72 cents per bucket of tomatoes—an 80 percent raise (the same two tons now yield the workers $90).

Different Industries, Same Abuses

Unfortunately, corporate farming is not the only industry in this country that engages in human rights abuses as well as employing a high rate of undocumented workers. In 2008, Sholom Rubashkin, an executive at Agriprocessors, a meatpacking plant in Iowa, was arrested for employing undocumented workers and helping them obtain fake identification.[16] Earlier in the year, a raid by Immigration and Customs Enforcement had arrested nearly 400 undocumented workers at Agriprocessors, including children as young as thirteen.[17] The workers who were arrested reported working seventeen hour shifts, six days a week; a lawyer representing many of the underage workers reported that some were too young to shave. Although the plant denied any knowledge of having employed underage workers, one youngster identified as Elmer L. told *The Dallas Morning News* that he had in fact informed his supervisors he was under eighteen years old. Elmer L. also reported being physically abused while working at Agriprocessors, including being kicked in the rear by a supervisor, which caused "a freshly sharpened knife to fly up and cut his elbow."[18]

In a similar vein, a twenty-two month investigation of a North Carolina poultry processor, House of Raeford, by *The Charlotte Observer* uncovered thirty-one confirmed injuries "serious enough to be recorded for regulators" by sampling workers living near the plant; less than 40 percent of the injuries had actually been logged by the company.[19] Among the injuries excluded from the logs were one worker's shattered ankle caused by a machine's faulty brakes, carpal tunnel syndrome causing intense pain and numbness (for which the employee was refused the right to see a doctor by a company nurse) and a cut with a knife leading to two missed days of work due to severe pain for another worker. Most amazingly, one House of Raeford plant recorded no musculoskeletal disorders—such as carpal tunnel and tendonitis, which are common at processing plants—between June 2003 and April 2007.[20] The plant employed 800 workers, including two who reported undergoing surgery for carpal tunnel at company expense during the period that no musculoskeletal disorders were logged. The plant's manager explained the lack of musculoskeletal disorders by saying that, "Hispanics are very good with their hands and working with a knife. We've gotten less complaints . . . it's more like a natural movement for them."[21]

It should come as no surprise that plants like House of Raeford are able to cover up worker injuries with relative ease, as inspections of plants in the poultry industry reached a 15-year low in 2008.[22] On the whole, plants are inspected less frequently and less comprehensively than they were in the past. In 2006, less than one plant in five was inspected, and as of 2008, some plants had not been inspected since 2000.[23] In addition, fines for serious violations average only $1,100, and it has been a decade since the U.S. Occupational Safety and Health Administration (OSHA) has fined any poultry processor for workplace hazards likely to cause musculoskeletal disorders. When questioned about their lax attitude towards the industry, OSHA officials cited the ever-decreasing numbers of reported injuries as proof that plants are safer than ever.[24]

The way to curb human rights abuses within slaughterhouses is not necessarily with new laws, but with a new outlook from government on its role in regulating business, something I hope we see from the Obama administration. While a plant hoping to abuse its employees as a means of increasing productivity and profits will of course find inspections burdensome, I think we would all agree that does not mean the inspections should not take place, nor does it mean that the company should not be fined for violations. And while the government should not intervene when businesses behave ethically on their own accord, the deregulatory environment of the past several decades often prevents the government from having the ability to intervene when businesses acts unethically. Finally, as with the case of Agriprocessors, we need to continue to arrest senior executives of plants that willfully violate laws by hiring and mistreating undocumented workers, because when the individuals at the top have something to lose personally by violating the law, they will be less likely to do so.

Animal Abuse and the PITS

While we have examined the physical and economic abuses that farm and plant workers suffer, one area that should not be overlooked is the psychological damage that these workers endure, particularly those directly involved in killing animals. Ed Van Winkle, a worker in a hog plant, said, "The worst thing, worse than the physical danger, is the emotional toll . . . Pigs down on the kill floor have come up and nuzzled me like a puppy. Two minutes later I had to kill them—beat them to death with a pipe. I can't care."[25] While research on the psychological impact of slaughterhouse workers is limited, a report written in 2007 Jennifer Dillard, then a student at the Georgetown University Law Center, suggests that employees may suffer from a form of post-traumatic stress disorder known as Perpetration-Induced Traumatic Stress (PITS).[26] The report states that "we have a common understanding that taking pleasure in the cruel death of a helpless animal is an antisocial and potentially psychotic characteristic," pointing to stories of slaughterhouse employees brutalizing animals "just for fun" as evidence that psychological harm may have occurred.[27]

While I do not see an obvious way for a slaughterhouse employee to perform his or her job without killing animals, if we were to curb some of the worst practices, perhaps we could help both the animals and the humans charged with killing them. The government already requires that "in the case of cattle, calves, horses, mules, sheep, swine, and other livestock, *all animals are [to be] rendered insensible to pain* by a single blow or gunshot or an electrical, chemical or other means that is rapid and effective, before being shackled, hoisted, thrown, cast, or cut." (This excludes animals being slaughtered in accordance with the ritual requirements of a religious faith).[28] Note that chickens and turkeys are excluded from this law.

The good news is that when the law is followed correctly, the animals' suffering is extremely brief during their last moments of life. Temple Grandin, a professor of animal science at Colorado State University, has done remarkable work designing facilities that allow animals to be handled, transported and slaughtered in ways that stress them as little as possible; nearly half of the cattle in the United States are slaughtered at facilities she designed.[29] The bad news is that the law often is not followed as slaughterhouse employees, with only seconds to stun an animal before it is hung upside down or scalded in hot water, simply cannot keep up with the speed of the modern line. As a basis of comparison, a century ago, a line would kill 50 cows an hour; now some kill up to 400 per hour.[30] In 2001, a video secretly made by workers at Iowa Beef Processors and reviewed by veterinarians for *The Washington Post* showed cattle that were still alive and conscious after being stunned, dangling upside down by a leg. More than twenty workers signed affidavits saying that the atrocities depicted in the video were commonplace and that their supervisors know about them. One employee, Martin Fuentes, told the *Post*, "I've seen thousands and thousands of cows go through the slaughter process alive. The cows can get seven minutes down the line and still be alive. I've been in the side-puller where they're still alive. All the hide is stripped out down the neck there."[31] In addition to being unspeakable cruel to the animals (as well as being illegal), allowing living cows to go through the slaughter process is also a hazard to employees, as Fuentes suffered a broken arm when a dying cow kicked him as it was being butchered alive.

There are two solutions to this problem. First, we must require that slaughterhouses slow down their line speeds to a rate at which workers can perform their duties safely and accurately. Second, we must examine the USDA's inspection practices, which shifted drastically upon the implementation of a quality control program known as HACCP (Hazard Analysis Critical Control Points or Have a Cup of Coffee and Pray, depending on who you ask). The program, begun in 1998, was intended to provide for better food safety, but instead allowed for greater corporate control of the quality insurance process and "rendered the USDA's humane slaughter enforcement program essentially nonexistent."[32] Clearly, it is time to reassess the HACCP program, and the USDA's inspection program as a whole to determine how we can best ensure that inspectors are able to do their jobs.

Also consider, as in the case of video unveiled by the Humane Society of the United States in 2008, the treatment of sick animals that arrive at the slaughterhouse unable to walk to their own deaths. The video showed workers "kicking cows, ramming them with the blades of a forklift, jabbing them in the eyes, applying painful electrical shocks and even torturing them with a hose and water," as they tried to force sick or injured animals to walk to slaughter. [33] A bill introduced in 1993, the Downed Animal Protection Act (H.R. 559) would have mandated that all animals unable to walk be "humanely euthanized" by a method that "rapidly and effectively renders the animal insensitive to pain." However, the bill did not pass.[34] Such a law, if passed—and enforced—is a reasonable anti-cruelty measure that could prevent many animals from suffering needlessly.

At the same time that Congress was debating the Downed Animal Protection Act in the mid-1990s, it was also considering the Humane Methods of Poultry Slaughter Act (H.R. 649). As poultry are currently excluded from the Humane Slaughter Act, accounts of poultry slaughter processes describe a wide range of brutalities. For example, poultry processors utilize throat-cutting machines that kill most of the birds, and employees are instructed to kill any birds missed by the machine. However, an undercover investigator for PETA reported "numerous birds that were scalded alive in the feather removal tank while they were still conscious and able to feel pain" at a Tyson plant in Heflin, Alabama.[35] The investigator brought this to management's attention and received a reply that it was an acceptable practice for up to forty birds per shift to be killed in this manner. Yet no disciplinary action was taken when it happened to more than forty birds in a shift. Passing and enforcing the Humane Methods of Poultry Slaughter Act, which requires that "poultry is rendered insensible to pain by electrical, chemical, or other means that is rapid and effective before or immediately after being shackled or otherwise prepared for slaughter" would represent an important step forward for the humane treatment of poultry.[36] (Like the Humane Slaughter Act, this law would also exempt animals that were being slaughtered in accordance with the ritual requirements of a religious faith).

In addition to ensuring that animals do not suffer in death, we should also do our best to prevent any needless suffering during their lives. In 2008, the state of California passed Proposition 2, a measure to improve the lives of veal calves, laying hens and breeding sows. All three animals are commonly confined to small spaces, and the new law requires allowing them enough space to "turn around, lie down, stand up, and fully extend their limbs."[37] While Proposition 2 only outlaws the very worst forms of maltreatment—other practices, like debeaking chickens, would draw public criticism if they were more widely discussed—veal crates, gestation crates for sows and battery cages for chickens do represent some of the worst practices within our livestock industry, so this is certainly a step forward. Hopefully, in future years we will see successful ballot initiatives in other states to outlaw these practices, as well as many others that are cruel to animals.

In the end, our standards for human and animal rights say a lot about who we are as a people. As Americans, we should not be willing to sacrifice the lives of farmworkers, or allow laying hens to live trapped in cages slightly larger than eight square inches or have any animal undergo torture at the slaughterhouse so that we can pay a few pennies less for our food.[38]

11. THE FARM BILL

"The Farm Bill" is the generic name given to a large piece of legislation that passes Congress every five to seven years and helps set agricultural and food policy for the United States. Since government support for farms, food assistance programs, agricultural trade, marketing and rural development policies are governed by a variety of different laws and agencies, the farm bill provides an "opportunity for lawmakers to address agricultural and food issues more comprehensively."[1] The very first farm bill—the Agricultural Adjustment Act of 1933—was passed under the administration of Franklin D. Roosevelt, while the most recent bill, passed last year, was named the Food, Conservation and Energy Act of 2008. The next farm bill is due to come before Congress in 2012.

The farm bill is not the only legislation relevant to food or agriculture; instead, it provides a blueprint for farm and food policy, while the USDA decides how these policies will be specifically implemented. At the same time that long-term policy is being set by the USDA, Congress passes annual agricultural appropriations bills, specifying which programs and agencies receive funding, and how much they will receive. Just because the farm bill says that a particular program or agency should receive money doesn't mean it will actually happen, as until Congress gives the green light in a separate appropriations bill, the money doesn't flow.

Even though we have several years to prepare for the next farm bill, it is important to start thinking about it now, so that we can call, write, fax and email the USDA to support positions and programs beneficial to sustainable agriculture, and so we are organized and ready once Congress takes up the next bill. However, we shouldn't focus only on the future; we also need to keep careful track of which programs received funding in the 2008 bill, so that we can make sure these programs are actually funded in the congressional appropriations bills.

History of the Farm Bill: Rise and Fall

With America in the throes of the Great Depression, the first farm bill was passed in 1933 primarily to manage fluctuations in commodity price and supply. In an unregulated market, farmers will always produce the maximum amount of commodities (crops like corn, soy, wheat, rice and cotton) possible. In years of abundance, supply will outweigh demand, meaning that prices will fall below the cost of production. Beginning with the first farm bill, and lasting until it was co-opted by agribusiness beginning in the 1970s, commodity policy in the United States managed supply as a means of keeping farmers solvent and ensuring a safe domestic food supply.

When the government sets a price floor and then removing excess supply from the market when the price would fall below that set floor, buyers of commodities (i.e. grain processors and livestock operations) will pay farmers a fair price for their crops. However, when the government shifts to a system that sets a target price and subsidizes farmers to make up the difference between the actual price and the target price, taxpayers pay the subsidies while agribusiness pays rock bottom commodity prices. Of course, there are exceptions—in years when demand surges or supply falls short, commodity prices naturally rise, easing the burden on taxpayers and increasing costs to agribusiness.

Commodity policy is set in the Farm Bill. The system as originally implemented allowed farmers to take out a loan from the government using their crops as collateral. Thus, the loan rate served as a de facto price floor (if the government would give you $3/bushel, then you wouldn't be willing to sell your crop for any less than that on the open market). If prices recovered, farmers could repay their loan to the government and sell their crops. If prices didn't recover, the farmers kept the money and the government got their crops which it could use for food aid. The government also managed overall supply by releasing farmers' crops taken as collateral onto the open market when supply fell short of demand. Commodity subsidies and supply management not only assisted farmers with low prices in years of surplus, it also shielded buyers of commodities and, ultimately consumers, from high prices in the event of a shortage.

The farm bills of recent decades have dismantled this system. In 1985, the government removed the price floor established by the loan rate, then went even further in the 1996 farm bill, the Freedom to Farm Act (a.k.a. the "Freedom to Fail" Act) when it tried to wean farmers off of subsidies altogether. However, without supply-management measures in place, the 1996 farm bill resulted in overproduction and low prices—sometimes prices even lower than production costs. While family farmers suffered under these circumstances, with their incomes stagnating or declining, the 1996 bill proved to be a boon for industrial livestock operations, which enjoyed lower feed prices.

The 1996 farm bill also ended acreage restrictions, land set-asides, and other programs intended to limit supply, leading to a 28 percent increase in corn production and a 42 percent increase in soy production.[2] After all was said and done, America was producing about 50 percent more crops than it was able to consume, and was forced to rely on exports to sell the surplus.[3] However, when the Asian Financial Crisis hit in 1997, export markets collapsed and prices followed, with corn dropping 32 percent and soy 21 percent.[4]

While commodity buyers were growing fatter from lower prices, farmers were rapidly losing their place in the economic food chain. By 2002, for every dollar spent on food by consumers, farmers only received 19 cents, down from 37 cents in 1980 and 47 cents in 1952.[5] When the farm share (the amount farmers receive of every dollar spent on food) decreases, it means that both farmers and consumers alike are losing ground, while those in the middle—processors, distributors, and retailers—are increasing their profits. In this case, consumers paid three times—in the form of taxes used to maintain a subsidy system that kept commodity prices low; when they bought processed foods; and when they paid for healthcare for their diet-related illnesses.

Back in 1975, Jim Hightower wrote that "The new agriculture is not calling for farmers, particularly not in decision-making positions. It is calling for the profit-sensitive executives of giant corporations." He went on to predict that consumers could "expect less of nature's own stuff and more conglomerate concoctions sold to you by means of brand-name identification."[6] While Hightower understood the direction our food system was heading in back in the 1970s, I wonder if he could have guessed the magnitude of changes that would occur over the next thirty years.

A MESS

The current farm bill is divided into fifteen sections, called titles: commodity programs, conservation, trade, nutrition, credit, rural development, research and related matter, forestry, energy, horticulture and organic agriculture, livestock (which was added in the 2008 bill), crop insurance and disaster assistance programs, commodity futures, miscellaneous and trade and tax provisions.[7] Despite the long list, most of the money in the bill is allocated to two titles: commodity programs and nutrition. The commodity programs title provides "income support, with new payment and eligibility limits, for wheat, feed grains, cotton, rice, oilseeds, and pulses through direct payments (except pulses), counter-cyclical payments, marketing loan assistance program, and new average crop revenue election payments."[8] Basically, it sets up a system to ensure we have lots of cheap corn, wheat, rice, soy and cotton so we can run factory farms and make processed foods.

The nutrition title expands "eligibility for Food Stamp Program, renamed Supplemental Nutrition Assistance Program… Increases funding for Emergency Food Assistance Program, Fresh Fruit and Vegetable Program, and Senior Farmers' Market Nutrition Program," as well as creating "initiatives for community food security, promoting locally produced foods, and healthy eating patterns, including curbing obesity."[9] While this may sound good on paper, in reality, the nutrition title serves to make sure that people eat all of those factory-farmed and processed foods. How is this so?

First, we must provide a definition of what "food" is in our current agricultural system. Hank Herrera, project manager for the HOPE Collaborative, an Oakland, California-based group dedicated to sustainable environmental change, defines food as an "edible plant or animal that grows, walks or swims on the earth and its waters with no genetic engineering, no hormone-driven growth and no synthetic chemical substances to mimic natural qualities." To Herrera, any other edible substance is a "manufactured edible substitute substance," or "MESS." A "MESS" has "ingredients that depend on genetic modification and genetic engineering, hormone and antibiotic residue from concentrated production and synthetic additives," which "subvert food cultures and food sovereignty….and contribute to the alarming toxic load that every human being now carries."[10]

Unfortunately, the current farm bill ensures the continued growth and manufacturing of MESSes, as well as the subsequent consumption of these MESSes by recipients of federal nutrition programs, such as food stamps. While the commodity program title legislates the creation of MESSes, the nutrition title, which governs a number of federal programs, makes the rules that promote MESS consumption. Among the programs the title governs are:[11]

- SNAP (formerly known as food stamps): Provides low income Americans with money on a debit card (called EBT—electronic benefits transfer) that can be used to purchase food.
- TEFAP (The Emergency Food Assistance Program): Provides food to food banks.
- CSFP (Commodity Supplemental Food Program): Provides food to low income women, infants, children and the elderly.
- Fruit and Vegetable Program: Distributes fresh (or dried) fruits and vegetables to elementary and secondary schools.
- Healthy Food Education and School Gardening Pilot Program: Creates hands on gardening programs at high-poverty schools. (This is currently only a pilot program, and is therefore unavailable in most states).
- Farmers Market Nutrition Programs: Provides pregnant and nursing mothers, infants, children under five and seniors with cash vouchers to buy produce at farmers' markets.*

All too often, these programs serve to transfer taxpayer dol-

---

*The two other major nutrition programs—the school lunch program and WIC (Women, Infants, and Children) are not included in the farm bill. Congress will reauthorize those programs in a Child Nutrition Reauthorization bill, most likely sometime in 2009.

lars into the pockets of Big Agriculture in return for the sale of MESSes to our nation's most vulnerable citizens. As an example of how this happens, let's take a look at a family of three who, by making below $22,884 pre-tax per year with no greater than $,2000 in assets, is eligible for SNAP.[12] The maximum SNAP benefit for this family would be $463 per month, or approximately $36 per person per week (a little over $5 per day). How can a person eat a balanced diet for $5 per day? In theory, by following the government-designed "Thrifty Food Plan" which the USDA uses to determine the financial level of the poverty line, which in turn determines SNAP eligibility. The plan specifies the amounts of various types of grains, vegetables, fruits, milk products, meat, beans and "other foods" by weight that an average person would need to eat, divided out by age and gender.[13] For example, a male between the ages of 19 and 50 would be allocated a total of 39.86 lbs of food per week, divided into 4.55 lbs of grains, 9.27 lbs of vegetables, 8.41 lbs of fruits, 11.37 lbs of milk products, 3.99 lbs of meat and beans and 2.26 lbs of "other foods" (coffee, soda, soup, frozen entrees, candy, condiments, etc). Since the government estimates the cost of food for each age and gender, the cost for this meal plan would be $40.20 per week.[14] However, this is the most expensive estimate for the thrifty plan, which assumes that small children cost as low as $20.80 per week and that women max out at $36.10.

The Thrifty Food Plan in of itself does not encourage MESS consumption. In fact, many of the foods included in the plan are actually quite healthy, including carrots, broccoli, spinach, green beans, a variety of whole grains, berries, melons, citrus, yogurt and other foods found in a healthy diet.[15] While the plan also includes pie, cookies, doughnuts, marshmallows and fudge, it clearly specifies that these empty calorie foods should make up a small part of one's diet.

That's the good news. The bad news is that families in many parts of the country simply cannot afford the healthy foods on the Thrifty Food Plan. A joint study conducted by Boston Medical Center and Drexel University found that a family of four following the Thrifty Food Plan would exceed their food stamp budget by $210 per month in Boston and by $263 per month in Philadelphia.[16] Perhaps there are parts of the country in which a low-income family on food stamps can afford the Plan, but this is not the case in large, expensive cities. And, what was worse than the high cost of food was the unavailability of many of the 104 items listed in the Thrifty Food Plan. For example, stores in low-income areas in Boston and Philadelphia lacked 16 percent and 38 percent of the items, respectively, with the most commonly missing items being fresh fruits and vegetables, whole grains, low fat dairy and fish and lean meats... in other words, the healthy stuff.[17]

Getting Rid of the MESS

How then do we change the food system to promote the growing and eating of healthy food instead of creating a MESS? To solve the problem of poor people not being able to afford healthy foods like fruits and vegetable, the government should provide incentives and assistance to establish grocery stores, cooperatives, and/or farmers' markets in underserved communities, and by equipping farmers' markets with EBT card readers so they can accept food stamps. For example, the Wholesome Wave foundation encourages healthy food choices by providing grants that double the value of food stamps when they are spent at farmers markets. In a Holyoke, Massachusetts market that received one of their grants, sales using food stamps increased 290 percent between August and October of 2008.[18] Expanding this program to all food stamp recipients nationwide would help promote fruit and vegetable consumption. And, assuming that many food stamp recipients also receive Medicaid, the increased costs to taxpayers in farmers' market foods would most likely be offset to a certain extent by decreased medical care costs.

In addition, the poverty threshold (and therefore, food stamp eligibility) is currently determined nationally instead of taking into account the cost of living in the place that a person actually lives. How can we assume that a family making $15,000 in New York City has the same standard of living as a family making the same amount in rural Nebraska? The government should therefore calibrate its Thrifty Food Plan (and food stamp eligibility and benefits) to accurately reflect people's real cost of living. Furthermore, when the government began calculating the poverty line using the Thrifty Food Plan in 1964, it assumed that a family would spend one-third of its income on food.[19] Today, however, families spend an average of 12.6 percent of their income on food. The government should update its calculation of the poverty line (which also determines eligibility for food stamps and other nutrition programs) to reflect the current percentage of household income spent on food.

On the agricultural side of the ledger, I received a glimpse into a possible sustainable future when I visited the Rodale Institute in Kutztown, Pennsylvania in 2008.[20] The Institute, which has performed decades of research on organic and conventional farming, had asked a neighboring farm for some of its conventional corn so that they could compare its nutritional value with that of organic corn. The neighboring farmer replied that they did not need to test his corn, because he already knew it was less nutritious; he added that he wasn't paid to grow nutritious corn—he was paid to grow as much "yellow stuff" as possible, as cheaply as possible. The oversupply of cheap "yellow stuff" is at the foundation of our current MESS. We need to find a way to reward farmers for best environmental practices, instead of rewarding them for the highest yield.

Timothy LaSalle, CEO of the Rodale Institute, has an idea for how we can accomplish this. The Institute has found that conventional agriculture degrades the soil, breaking down the soil's carbon into carbon dioxide (a greenhouse gas). However, organic agriculture—when done right—regenerates the soil. As the soil regenerates, it sequesters carbon from the atmosphere, which means that regenerative agricultural techniques may offer a possible solution to global warming. LaSalle recommends rewarding farmers for carbon sequestration, an idea that makes perfect sense in the context of any cap and trade system designed to reduce greenhouse gas emissions. If one must pay for the right to emit carbon, why shouldn't we reward those who sequester it? Paying farmers for carbon sequestration would be like paying homeowners with solar panels for selling electricity back to the grid. And, for every two acres under organic cultivation, the reductive effect on global warming would be as if one car was taken off the road.[21] Overall, organic agriculture, if practiced on all tillable land globally, could sequester nearly 40 percent of all current carbon dioxide emissions.[22]

To understand how this all works, recall that plants use the sun's energy to combine carbon dioxide and water to create carbohydrates. When plant matter decays and becomes part of the soil, the soil holds the carbon that was once part of the plant. Back in the 1950s, soil in this country was often as much as twenty percent carbon; now most soil is between one and two percent carbon.[23] Not surprisingly, industrial agriculture techniques are responsible for the fifty year degradation of our soil. However, when we allow organic matter to break down and form new soil, we increase the amount of carbon in the soil. The trick for modern farmers is to do this in an economically viable way. Not all organic farmers do this, by the way. While some may abstain from using pesticides and fertilizers that are not permitted by the USDA National Organic Program, if they replace those chemicals with frequent tilling or other practices that do not build up the soil, they are not helping to fight global warming.

The techniques pioneered by the Rodale Institute are fully compatible with contemporary agricultural methods. Even if a farmer currently grows corn and soy over thousands of acres, he or she can continue to do so using Rodale's recommended farming methods without sacrificing crop yield. While farmers will suffer lower yields during the first few years after they stop using chemical inputs because their soil will not yet have the biodiversity necessary to help their crops thrive, by the five year mark, organics will produce yields equal to conventional agriculture, and after that will produce higher yields in most years than conventional agriculture would.

In addition to its potential effects on carbon sequestration, the methods at Rodale may also lead to a dramatic reduction in fossil fuel energy use. According to the research of David Pimentel, professor of ecology and agriculture at Cornell University and a leading expert on agriculture and energy, a conventional corn production system requires 231.7 gallons of diesel per acre (199.2 gallons of diesel per acre if the land is not tilled). However, in an organic system, only 121.6 gallons of diesel are required (77.5 gallons of diesel per acre if the land is not tilled).[24] Thus, a farmer switching from conventional methods with tillage to no-till organic methods would experience a two-thirds reduction in his or her fuel needs.

To translate Rodale's work into policy, LaSalle and others are looking for a simple method to quantify the amount of carbon a farmer has sequestered in the soil so that the government can establish a system to compensate farmers. With a way to measure carbon sequestration, Congress would be able to supplant current yield-based subsidies with payments for carbon sequestration. Farmers who sequester carbon could then reduce pollution by fertilizer run-off, build biodiversity and cultivate nutrient-rich soil (and thus, nutrient-rich food), while at the same time boosting crop yields.

These ideas are actually consistent with an already existing program: the Conservation Stewardship Program, or CSP. First created in 2002, CSP is a conservation program for land that is under cultivation.[25] Conservation "reserve" programs compensate farmers who allow land that is valuable as animal habitats to remain untouched. Unfortunately, these programs are chronically underfunded, so even if every farmer in America wanted to get on board with them, they would not all be eligible to receive federal money. As a consequence, instead of conserving, farmers continue to oblige federal policy by producing as much as possible, as cheaply as possible, with conventional techniques.

The Livestock Title

Even though laws like the Packers and Stockyards Act of 1921 and the Agricultural Fair Practices Act of 1967 were designed to enforce fair, competitive markets for livestock, it is clear that, after several decades of deregulation, the current system is broken. Livestock markets have become highly consolidated oligopolies, and independent farmers and ranchers face more challenges to compete than ever before. As a result, with the support of over 170 organizations including the Western Organization of Resource Councils, R-CALF USA, RAFI-USA, the National Farmers Union, the Sustainable Agriculture Coalition, the Organization for Competitive Markets, and the Center for Rural Affairs, Senate Agriculture Committee Chairman Tom Harkin was able to take the lead and include the first ever livestock title in the Senate version of the 2008 farm bill. From there, the conference committee that combined the House and Senate versions also included the livestock title, making the title part of the final bill.

Understanding why this title is so important—and why it needs to be improved dramatically in the next farm bill—first requires an understanding of the livestock market. In particular, the beef market is a good example as it is the most consolidated of the industry. Typically, cows are raised from the time they are born until they reach a weight of between 500 and 800 lbs in what are known as "cow-calf" operations. These operations, located on thousands of independently owned ranches throughout the country, allow calves to live relatively natural lives, nursing on their mothers' milk and grazing on pasture.[26] Once they reach either "feeder cattle" (500 lbs) or "yearling" weight (about 750 to 800 lbs), the cow-calf operations can either sell their cattle and/ or yearlings to feedlots, or else retain ownership while at the same time paying for the cattle's room and board at the feedlot.[27] If the cow-calf operations choose to sell their cattle to the feedlots, the price they receive is based on the current market price for slaughter-weight cattle.

The cows remain in the feedlots until they reach slaughter-weight, at which point they are sold to meat packers. The meat packers have a set capacity to slaughter cattle, based on the number of plants they own; this determines demand. The meat packers fill this demand with cattle from three sources: their own "captive supply" (cattle they already control either via contract or ownership); feedlot cattle; and worn out dairy cattle. When the meat packers are able fill their demand mostly with captive supply, the demand for cattle from the other two sources diminishes. By comparing their demand with the supply of feedlot cattle, excluding captive supply, meat packers arrive at the market price they are willing to pay for slaughter-weight cattle. This price then helps determine the price for worn out dairy cattle. One thing to keep in mind about the determination of the market price is that it is not economically viable to transport slaughter-weight cattle beyond a distance of 250 miles, so for example, a feedlot in Illinois cannot sell its animals to a packing plant in California because the local plants are not willing to pay a reasonable price.

The call for fairness in the beef industry refers in large part to the ability of a feedlot or a rancher to sell their finished cattle to a packer at a fair price. In theory, when several packers are competing to purchase enough finished cattle to meet their demand, the result should be a fair market price. However, since there are so few packers competing for cattle and their demand is reduced due to captive supply, they can effectively drive the price down. Furthermore, a feedlot or rancher has only two weeks once a cow reaches slaughter-weight to sell the cow or else it will sell for a reduced price because it has become too fat.[28]

The reason there is so little competition for cattle is because of the mass consolidation in the beef industry. The top four meat packers in the United States are JBS Swift, National Beef, Tyson and Cargill. Together, these four companies own twenty-three plants in the U.S., mostly in Nebraska, Kansas, Texas, Colorado, and Pennsylvania[29] and control nearly 95 percent of slaughter-ready steers and heifers in this country.[30] Such consolidation is not unique to the beef industry; the hog and chicken industries are similarly concentrated. In 2007, the top four pork packers were Smithfield, Tyson, Swift & Co and Cargill, who together controlled nearly 66 percent of the industry.[31]* The top four in the broiler industry (Pilgrim's Pride, Tyson, Perdue and Sanderson) controlled 58.5 percent of the market in 2007.[32]

When consolidation gives a few powerful companies control over an entire market, these companies are then able use their economies of scale to pressure small competitors.[33] In other words, if we care about the fate of the little guys, we need to prevent consolidation and the anti-competitive behavior it encourages. Unfortunately, advocates for fair competition fought for, but ultimately lost, a "packer ban" in the 2008 farm bill, which would have banned packer ownership of cattle more than fourteen days prior to slaughter. Each day, the four largest beef packers slaughter up to 106,500 head of cattle.[34] Since these companies already control up to 35 percent of that number (up to about 41,400) in captive supply, they only need to bid competitively for 65,000 cattle instead of bidding for all 106,500. The packer ban would have eliminated the loss of competition from the 20 to 35 percent of pre-slaughter cattle that the largest beef packers control as captive supply.[35] While enacting the ban would not have re-

---

* This information is already out of date, as JBS and Swift merged in 2007 and JBS Swift announced a merger with Smithfield in 2008.

stored full competitive balance to the market, it would certainly have been an improvement over the current situation.

Overall, restoring competition to livestock markets goes beyond the farm bill. What we need are not necessarily new laws, but for government to enforce the ones already on the books that were designed to prevent or eliminate anti-competitive behavior, such as the Packers and Stockyards Act. Allowing mergers between large companies in already-concentrated industries is hardly the way to promote fairness. Additionally, it is hard to ask a farmer to use more eco-friendly practices or to treat his or her animals more humanely when rising feed costs and low prices are squeezing him or her on both ends. Similarly, it makes little economic sense to ask a farmer to grow corn in a more sustainable manner when the market rewards nothing but yield. On the other end of the chain, it is absurd under the present system to ask a family earning poverty-level wages to use its $1 per meal from food stamps on organic, local vegetables.

Ultimately, the winners in the current system are Big Oil, Big Ag, Big Pharma and Big Food. Farmers buy seeds, oil, equipment, fertilizer and pesticides from enormous companies, then sell their crops to other enormous companies. From there, the crops become animal feed (and subsequently meat, eggs, and dairy), processed foods and fuel, which are sold to consumers by retailers. Restructuring the next farm bill to reward regenerative agricultural practices, provide aid to those in need so they can buy healthy foods and promote fairness in the livestock industry, will bring us closer to realizing the goal of having a truly sustainable food system.

CONCLUSION

Now that you have finished reading my "recipe for America," I imagine you are asking yourself one question in particular: Can we do it? Can we turn our currently unsustainable food system, a system that is unfair to workers, bad for our health, cruel to animals and destructive to our environment, into one that treats workers fairly, respects human and animal rights, nourishes our bodies and renews the land? While none of the ideas I have talked about in this book will happen all by themselves, with a strong, organized and sustained effort from citizens who are tired of a food system that profits the few at the expense of the many, we can make a sustainable food system a reality.

At the same time, while this book lays out a plan for a sustainable food system, what I propose is just a starting point, and is certainly not designed to take us all the way to where we need to go. For one thing, when it comes to food, the future is always uncertain, as it is difficult to anticipate the next trick the corporate food industry has up its sleeve. (Who would have thought that feedlots would respond to high corn prices by feeding their cattle potato chips and M&Ms?[1]) New problems crop up all the time, and it's up to us in the sustainable food movement to decide when and how to take action. While the Obama administration is far friendlier to our goals than the Bush administration was, the House Agriculture Committee, which is responsible for much of the food policy in this country, is not at all hospitable to the needs of sustainable agriculture, as all but a few of the Democrats on the committee are what are known as "Blue Dog Dems"—business-friendly Democrats who do not support the goals of the sustainable agriculture movement. (Recall how the House Agriculture committee chairman, Collin Peterson, once called consumers who paid extra for local or organic food "dumb.") Even though his Senate counterpart, Tom Harkin, is a strong advocate for organics, children's health and conservation, any bill that passes the Senate must be reconciled with Peterson's House version and then passed by both Houses of Congress, allowing Peterson and his committee to single-handedly present a major roadblock to reform.

If, as citizens and activists, we do nothing, we will get nothing in return from our government. This is where you come in. In the appendix to this book, you will find an activist tool kit that offers specific instructions on how you can stay informed on the issues that affect sustainable agriculture, and shows you how to put pressure on government and industry to help reform our food system. Activism is easy—when you have the right tools. For example, you can sign up for a mailing list that lets you know when there's an issue before Congress that you need to take action on. These lists enable you instantly send letters to your elected representatives, allowing you to get involved with the click of a mouse. If you have the time to do more, you can edit—thus personalizing—the letter before sending it, and encourage friends to send letters as well. While the act of a single individual contacting the government may seem insignificant, when members of Congress receive emails from hundreds or thousands of people concerning an issue, they listen. And, if you're willing to do even more, there are many other ways to get involved. The point is that it is easy, even for a busy person, to participate in our democracy and to influence the policy that is made in Washington or in our state capitols.

In the end, I hope that Recipe for America has revealed the sorry state our food system is currently in, and, more importantly, offered a vision of where it needs to go and how you can help get it there. Ultimately, it's all up to us—we can't wait for Coca-Cola and McDonald's, or the government, to come to the realization that they are harming people's health. They already know they are doing that—and they don't care. The big food corporations have lobbyists in Washington D.C. and in every state in the nation. If our legislators don't hear from us, loudly, they will not realize that there is another point of view besides that of Big Ag, and they will certainly not know that we are paying attention to their actions and holding them accountable for their votes.

Please join me in taking back our food system, and our democracy.

APPENDIX: HOW TO COOK UP A RECIPE FOR AMERICA

Sign Up to Receive Action Alerts

The fastest and easiest way to get involved politically in the sustainable food movement is to sign up for the mailing lists of organizations that send out action alerts. These organizations will do the hard work, researching issues, monitoring Congress and writing talking points. You can then get involved by filling in your name and contact information, customizing their letters if you want to, and, with a click of your mouse, you can send an email to members of Congress or the USDA.

Organizations I recommend include:
- Organic Consumers Association:
  http://www.organicconsumers.org
- Food and Water Watch:
  http://www.foodandwaterwatch.org
- Consumers Union: http://www.consumersunion.org
- Union of Concerned Scientists: http://www.ucsusa.org
- The Cornucopia Institute: http://www.cornucopia.org
- Food Democracy Now: http://www. fooddemocracynow. org

Follow Issues on Blogs

There are a number of blogs that follow food-related issues. While you should check out the nationally oriented blogs, you can also try and find out if there is a regional blog that follows local issues in your area. (And if no such blog exists, maybe you should start one!)

The food blogs I follow include:

- My blog, La Vida Locavore: http://www.lavidalocavore.org
- Marion Nestle's blog, Food Politics: http://www.food-politics.com
- The Ethicurean: http://www.ethicurean.com
- Obama Foodorama: http://obamafoodorama.blogspot.com
- U.S. Food Policy: http://usfoodpolicy.blogspot.com/
- Center for a Livable Future: http://www.livablefuture-blog.com
- Civil Eats: http://civileats.com
- Fooducate: http://www.fooducate.com/blog
- Consumers Union's blog, Not In My Food: http://www.consumersunion.org/blogs/nimf
- Change.org's Sustainable Food blog: http://food.change.org
- Grist's Food Kingdom: http://www.grist.org/kingdom/food
- The Green Fork blog: http://blog.eatwellguide.org
- Take a Bite Out of Climate Change: http://www.takeabite.cc/blog

Track Legislation

There is a fantastic site called Govtrack (http://www.govtrack.us) that allows anyone to create a free account and track specific bills, members of Congress, or House or Senate committees. I use this site to keep tabs on several congressional committees as well as to stay informed on any bill related to food or agriculture. Many states also offer tracking systems on their own sites.

Watch Congressional Hearings

One of the best ways to keep up with what is going on in Congress is by watching their committee hearings at http://www.house.

gov or http://www.senate.gov (select the appropriate committee to navigate to its website). Most committees post live webcasts of their hearings online and some also post archived webcasts of past hearings. Many committees deal with issues related to food and agriculture. As of 2009, the following committees covered topics related to food:

- House Energy & Commerce: Food safety
- House Agriculture: Food safety, obesity, the farm economy, NAIS
- Senate Agriculture: Child nutrition
- Senate Foreign Relations: Global hunger

Additionally, the Senate HELP committee (Health, Education, Labor and Pensions) held a hearing on childhood obesity in 2008, and I expect that the House Education and Labor committee will hold hearings on child nutrition sometime in 2009. After you watch a hearing, you can follow up by sending your Senators or Representative an email offering them your opinion on the issue—especially if they are on the committee that held the hearing.

Write A Letter to the Editor

When you see an article about food in the newspaper, write letter to the editor of the paper. If the paper covered the issue well, let them know and perhaps expand on their points. If they provided misinformation, tell them why they were mistaken and explain the truth. Try to keep your letters shorter than 150 words and always follow the instructions the newspaper provides (for example, they might ask you to include your home address and phone number) so your letter will have the best chance of being printed.

ACKNOWLEDGEMENTS

First and foremost, I would like to thank my publishers for the most amiable and positive professional relationship I've ever experienced, and for their brilliant work in guiding me through this process and editing my book. I feel my writing is like a model who is made up by hair and makeup artists but then gets the credit for her beauty. Like a made-up model, this book would not be half as beautiful without the fantastic work of Robert Lasner and Elizabeth Clementson, even though the cover gives the credit for it to me.

Second, I want to thank those in the sustainable food movement who have mentored me, inspired me, and educated me either personally or through their research and writing. Those people include: Marion Nestle, Ellen Fried, Kerry Trueman, Judith and Mike McGeary, Mark Winne, Michele Simon, George Naylor, Jim Goodman, Tom Philpott, John Peck, Destin Joy Layne, Deb Eschmeyer, Elanor Starmer, Steph Larsen, Natasha Chart, Tom Laskawy, Eddie Gehmen Kohan, Nicole de Beaufort, Dave Murphy, Anna Lappé, Naomi Starkman, Irene Lin, Christopher Cook, Hank Herrera, Rick North, Michael Pollan, and too many others to name.

I also owe a big thank you to the blogosphere, particularly

those on DailyKos and La Vida Locavore who have become my true family and my best friends in the past several years. You guys made me what I am and you are 100 percent responsible for this book. You believed in me more than I believed in myself at times, and because of your love and support, I was able to believe that I could write a book and then I was able to follow through and do it. In particular, thank you to JayInPortland, Asinus Asinum Fricat, Eddie C, TheFatLadySings, Dallasdoc, Land of Enchantment, and Desmoinesdem. And of course, thank you to Markos for creating DailyKos, without which I could have never discovered my passion for writing or connected with others who care about sustainable food and progressive politics around the U.S. and the world.

Thank you to Jonny Dexter, who wandered into the world of sustainable food with me back when it first captivated me, and who found it just as fascinating, delicious, and crucial to the health of our people and our environment as I do.

Last, thanks to my brother Adam, for loving me during his brief twenty-three years on this planet. I know you were proud of me for writing a book and you wanted to be here when it was finally finished. I wish you could have read it too.

NOTES

INTRODUCTION

1. My own calculation is based on USDA data that 4.1% of U.S.-produced corn is used for high fructose corn syrup, Ephraim Leibtag, "Corn Prices Near Record High, But What About Food Costs?," *Amber Waves*, February 2008, http://www.ers.usda.gov/AmberWaves/February08/Features/CornPrices.htm and the 2007 Census of Agriculture.

1. FROM EATER TO ACTIVIST

1. Tara Parker-Pope "The Farmers' Market Effect," *New York Times* Blog, January 15, 2008, http://well.blogs.nytimes.com/2008/01/15/the-farmers-market-effect/ (accessed March 1, 2008).

2. James Ridgeway, "Heritage Foundation on Hunger: Let Them Eat Broccoli," *Mother Jones*, December 3, 2007, http://www.motherjones.com/washington_dispatch/2007/12/hunger-let-them-eat-broccoli.html (accessed December 9, 2008).

3. Mari Gallagher Research & Consulting Group, *Examining the Impact of Food Deserts on Public Health in Chicago*, (Chicago: 2006).

4. Ibid., 2.

5. Center for Disease Control, "Behavioral Risk Factor Surveillance System," http://www.cdc.gov/brfss/.

6. Suzi Parker, "Finger-Lickin' Bad: How Poultry Producers are Ravaging the Rural South," *Grist*, February 21, 2006, http://www.grist.org/news/maindish/2006/02/21/parker/ (accessed December 13, 2008).

2. THE NOT-SO-GREEN REVOLUTION

1. Local Food and Value Added Conference, Eau Claire, WI, January 24, 2008.

2. Ann Vileisis, *Kitchen Literacy: How We Lost Knowledge of Where Food Comes from and Why We Need to Get It Back*, (Washington D.C.: Island

Press, 2008).

3. U.S. State Department of Agriculture Cooperative State Research, Education, and Extension Service, "Partnerships," http://www.csrees.usda.gov/qlinks/extension.html.

4. Ibid.

5. U.S. Departmennt of Agriculture, Cooperative State Research, Education, and Extension Service, "About Us," http://www.csrees.usda.gov/qlinks/extension.html (Accessed January 17, 2009).

6. Christopher D. Cook, *Diet for a Dead Planet: Big Business and the Coming Food Crisis*, (New York: The New Press, 2006), p. 102.

7. Ibid.

8. Ibid., 160.

9. Edmund Russell, *War and Nature: Fighting Humans and Insects with Chemicals from World War I to Silent Spring*, (New York, NY: Cambridge University Press, 2001).

10. Ibid., 6.

11. GlobalSecurity.org, "Chemical Corps", Alexandria, Virginia, http://www.globalsecurity.org/military/agency/army/chem.htm

12. Ibid.

13. Ibid.

14. Russell, *War and Nature*, 91-92.

15. Russell, *War and Nature*, 39, 55.

16. Edmund P. Russell, "Speaking of Annihilation": Mobilizing for War Against Human and Insect Enemies, 1914-1945," *Journal of American History* 82, no. 4 (March 1996): 15-16.

17. Russell, *War and Nature*, 86.

18. Ibid., 127.

19. Ibid., 147.

20. Ibid., 163.

21. Ibid., 155.

22. Ibid., 154.

23. Ibid., 202.

24. Ibid., 166.

25. Rachel Carson, *Silent Spring*, (Houghton Mifflin: New York,1962), 46-48.

26. Ibid., 46-48.

27. Ibid., 16.

28. Ibid., 15-32.

29. Ibid., 22.

30. Russell, *War and Nature*, 229.

31. Mark Arax and Jeanne Brokaw, "No Way Around Roundup," *Mother Jones*, January/February 1997, http://www.motherjones.com/news/feature/1997/01/brokaw.html (accessed February 23, 2008).

32. Ibid.

33. Bette Hilleman, "Atrazine Disrupts Frog Development: Exposure to Weed Killer Induces Hermaphroditism in Male Tadpoles," *Chemical & Engineering News*, April 22, 2002, http://pubs.acs.org/cen/critter/frogs2.html (accessed January 31, 2009).

34. U.S. Environmental Protection Agency, Pesticides: Re-registration, "Atrazine Updates", November 24th, 2008, http://www.epa.gov/pesticides/reregistration/atrazine/atrazine_update.htm (accessed January 31, 2009).

35. Carson, *Silent Spring*, 30-31.

36. Carol Kaesuk Yoon, "A 'Dead Zone' Grows in the Gulf of Mexico," *New York Times*, January 20, 1998, http://www.nytimes.com/1998/01/20/science/a-dead-zone-grows-in-the-gulf-of-mexico.html (accessed February 15, 2008).

37. John Roach, "Gulf of Mexico 'Dead Zone' Is Size of New Jersey," *National Geographic News*, May 25, 2005.

38. U.S. Environmental Protection Agency website, Region 7 Concentrated Animal Feeding Operations (CAFOs), "What is a CAFO?", February 27th, 2008, http://www.epa.gov/region7/water/cafo/index.htm

39. Ibid.

40. Pew Commission on Industrial Farm Animal Production, *Putting Meat on the Table: Industrial Farm Animal Production in America: Executive Summary*, August 2008, http://www.ncifap.org/_images/PCIFAPSmry.pdf, 9

41. Ibid.

42. Ibid.

43. Senate Committee on Government Affairs, *Testimony of Richard J. Dove, Waterkeeper Alliance*, 107th Cong., 2nd sess., March 13, 2002, http://hsgac.senate.gov/031302dove.htm (accessed February 13, 2008).

44. Natural Resources Defense Council, "Facts about Pollution from Livestock Farms," July 15, 2005, http://www.nrdc.org/water/pollution/ffarms.asp (accessed February 13, 2008).

45. "Pew Commission on Industrial Farm Animal Production, *Putting Meat on the Table: Industrial Farm Animal Production in America: Executive Summary*, 25.

46. Senate Committee on Government Affairs, *Testimony of Richard J.*

Dove, Waterkeeper Alliance.

47. Ibid.

48. Gary Onan, "From Pig to Plate", Presentation at the Local Food and Value Added Conference, Eau Claire, WI, January 24, 2008.

49. Robert Segelken, "CU and USDA: Cattle Feeding Change Could Cut E. Coli Risk," *Cornell Chronicle*, September 17, 1998, http://www.news.cornell.edu/Chronicle/98/9.17.98/cattle_feeding.html (accessed February 16, 2008).

50. Ibid.

51. Curtis W. Stofferahn, *Industrialized Farming and Its Relationship to Community Well-Being: An Update of a 2000 Report by Linda Lobao*, Prepared for the State of North Dakota, Office of the Attorney General for case *State of North Dakota v. Crosslands* North Dakota District Court, September 2006, www.und.nodak.edu/org/ndrural/Lobao%20&%20Stofferahn.pdf, 7.

52. Ibid.

53. David Ward, phone conversation, February 15, 2008.

54. Cook, *Diet for a Dead Planet*, 187.

55. Ibid.

56. Tom Philpott, "Farm Bill: Stick It To Big Meat: Back Under Debate in the Senate, the Farm Bill Lurches Ahead," Gristmill Blog, December 7, 2007, http://gristmill.grist.org/story/2007/12/7/8241/55183 (accessed February 15, 2008).

57. Institute of Medicine, "Childhood Obesity in the United States: Facts and Figures: Fact Sheet", September 2004, 1, http://www.iom.edu/File.aspx?ID=22606.

58. American Heart Association, "Statistical Fact Sheet-Risk Factor: Overweight and Obesity–Statistics", 2008, http://www.americanheart.org/downloadable/heart/1197994908531FS16OVR08.pdf (accessed February 1, 2009).

59. Paul Krugman, "Runaway Health Care Costs – We're #1!," *New York Times*, March 28, 2008, http://krugman.blogs.nytimes.com/2008/03/28/runaway-health-care-costs-were-1/ (accessed February 1, 2009).

60. Angie Tagtow, "Vilsack and Daschle Must Work Together in the New Year-Make Soil to Health Resolutions," La Vida Locavore, December 18, 2008, http://www.lavidalocavore.org/showDiary.do?diaryId=708 (accessed February 1, 2009).

61. Kerry O'Brien, "Pollan warns our diet is killing us," *The 7.30 Report*, May 27, 2008, http://www.abc.net.au/7.30/content/2007/s2257391.htm

(accessed February 1, 2009).

62. Blair Murray, "CLA Could Spell Success," Ontario Ministry of Agriculture Food & Rural Affairs, November 2001, http://www.omafra.gov.on.ca/english/livestock/dairy/facts/cla.htm (accessed February 3, 2009).

63. T.R. Dhiman, C.S. Poulson, D. Cornforth, and D.R. ZoBell, "Conjugated Linoleic Acid (CLA) and Vitamin E Levels in Pasture Forages for Beef Cattle," Utah State University, March 2006, http://extension.usu.edu/files/publications/publication/AG_Beef_2006-03.pdf (accessed February 3, 2009).

64. Matthew Cimitile, "Crops Absorb Livestock Antibiotics, Science Shows," *Environmental Health News*, January 6, 2009, http://www.environmentalhealthnews.org/ehs/news/antibiotics-in-crops (accessed February 1, 2009).

65. Centers for Disease Control and Prevention, "MRSA: Methicillin-resistant Staphylococcus aureus in Healthcare Settings," October 17, 2007, http://www.cdc.gov/Features/MRSA/ (accessed February 1, 2009).

66. Andrew Schneider, "Secret Ingredients," *Seattle Post-Intelligencer*, January 23, 2009, http://blog.seattlepi.nwsource.com/secretingredients/archives/160278.asp (accessed February 1, 2009).

67. Amy R. Sapkota, Lisa Y. Lefferts, Shawn McKenzie, and Polly Walker, "What Do We Feed to Food Production Animals? A Review of Animal Feed Ingredients and Their Potential Impacts on Human Health," (National Institute of Environmental Health Services, February 8, 2007).

3. SUSTAINABLE AGRICULTURE

1. John Ikerd, as quoted by Richard Duesterhaus in "Sustainability's Promise," *Journal of Soil and Water Conservation* 45, no.1 (Jan.-Feb. 1990): 4.

2. U.S. Department of Agriculture National Agriculture Library, "Sustainable Agriculture: Information Access Tools," March 18, 2009, http://www.nal.usda.gov/afsic/pubs/agnic/susag.shtml

3. Nodji Van Wychen (Farm tour, city, WI, July 29, 2006).

4. National Family Farm Coalition, "Who We Are," http://www.nffc.net/Who%20We%20Are/page-whoweare.htm

5. National Family Farm Coalition, "What We Stand For," http://www.nffc.net/What%20We%20Stand%20For/page-whatwestandfor.htm

6. Soil Foodweb, Inc., "Benefits of a Healthy Food Web," http://www.soilfoodweb.com/03_about_us/approach_pgs/a_01_benefits.html

7. Jeff Lowenfels and Wayne Lewis, *Teaming with Microbes: A Gardener's*

Guide to the Soil Food Web, (Portland, Oregon: Timber Press, 2006), 20-23.

8. Allan Savory, *Holistic Management: A New Framework for Decision Making*, (Washington, DC: Island Press, 1999).

9. Ibid., 141.

10. Ibid., 153.

11. "Market Gardening," *Mother Earth News*, May/June 1987, http://www.motherearthnews.com/Organic-Gardening/1987-05-01/Market-Gardening.aspx?page=2 (accessed February 21, 2008).

12. Eric Schlosser, *Reefer Madness* (New York: Houghton Mifflin, 2003), 80.

13. Andrew C. Revkin, "U.S. Requests Exemptions To Ozone Pact For Chemical," *New York Times*, March 4, 2004, http://query.nytimes.com/gst/fullpage.html?res=9F03E3DF133FF937A35750C0A9629C8B63&st=cse&sq=U.S.+Requests+Exemptions+To+Ozone+Pact+For+Chemical&scp=1 (accessed February 21, 2008).

14. Savory, *Holistic Management*, 38.

4. YES, I'VE HEARD THE ONE ABOUT 'WHOLE PAYCHECK'

1. California Certified Organic Farmers, http://ccof.org/

2. Harry MacCormack, phone interview on March 4, 2008.

3. Organic Trade Association, "Organic Foods Production Act Backgrounder," http://www.ota.com/pp/legislation/backgrounder.html

4. Ibid.

5. Michael Pollan, *The Omnivore's Dilemma*, (New York: Penguin Press USA, 2006), 160.

6. Phil Howard, "Buying Organic," *Good*, March/April 2008, 80-81.

5. LIVING LA VIDA LOCAVORE

1. Rev. Dr. Arvid Straube, Sermon delivered at First Unitarian Universalist Church of San Diego "Eat, Love, and Prayer--Making the Most of Thanksgiving," November 18, 2007, http://www.firstuusandiego.org/Uploads/Eat,%20Love,%20and%20Prayer_%20Making%20the%20Most%20of%20Thanksgiving.mp3

2. Ibid.

3. Marion Nestle, "Ask Marion: The Food Revolution," August 22, 2007, DailyKos, http://www.dailykos.com/story/2007/8/22/171958/195/412/374879

4. Ibid.

5. U.S. Department of Agriculture Report on Supply Chain and Food

Marketing 2008.

6. Chef's Collaborative, "About, " 2007, http://chefscollaborative.org/about/ (Accessed May 10, 2008).

7. Andrew and Robin Schiff, interview by author, San Diego, CA, March 22, 2008.

8. Bee Wilson, "The Last Bite: Is the World's Food System Collapsing?" *The New Yorker*, May 19, 2008, http://www.newyorker.com/arts/critics/atlarge/2008/05/19/080519crat_atlarge_wilson?currentPage=2 (Accessed May 14, 2008).

9. Community Food Security Coalition Conference Field Trip, Lancaster, PA, October 4, 2008.

10. Slow Food International, http://www.slowfood.com/

11. Alice Gomstyn, "Cheap Food in the City? Grow Your Own: City Dwellers Seeking to Save Money on Food Flock to Community Gardens," *ABC News*, June 4, 2008, http://abcnews.go.com/Business/Economy/story?id=4991251&page=1 (accessed June 7, 2008).

12. Barbara Miner, "An Urban Farmer is Rewarded for His Dream," *New York Times*, September 5, 2008, http://www.nytimes.com/2008/10/01/dining/01genius.html (accessed February 21, 2009).

13. Esther Sung, "Alice Waters and the Edible Schoolyard: A Book about Inspiration from the Ground Up," *Epicurious.com*, February 25, 2009, http://shine.yahoo.com/channel/food/alice-waters-and-the-edible-schoolyard-a-book-about-inspiration-from-the-ground-up-396986/ (accessed March 3, 2009).

14. Eddie Gehmen Kohan, "The FLOTUS Factor: Maria Shriver Announces Plans for an Edible Garden," Obama Foodorama, March 25, 2009, http://obamafoodorama.blogspot.com/2009/03/flotus-factor-maria-shriver-announces.html (Accessed March 25, 2009).

15. National Farm to School Program, http://www.farmtoschool.org/index.php (accessed March 3, 2009).

16. National Farm to School Network, "Nourishing the Nation One Tray at a Time: Farm to School Initiatives in the Child Nutrition Reauthorization," February 2009.

6. BARRIERS TO BUILDING A SUSTAINABLE FOOD SYSTEM

1. Amory Starr, Adrian Card, Carolyn Benepe, Garry Auld, Dennis Lamm, Ken Smith, and Karen Wilken, "Sustaining Local Agriculture: Barriers and Opportunities to Direct Marketing Between Farms and Restaurants in Colorado," *Agriculture and Human Values*, 2003, 301-321 .

2. Ibid., 311.

3. Jennifer Langston, "Many Barriers Keep Fresh, Organic Food Out of School Lunches," *Seattle Post-Intelligencer*, October 15, 2007, http://seattlepi.nwsource.com/local/335486_farmtoschool15.html

4. Ibid.

5. Ibid.

6. Barry Yeoman, "Unhappy Meals," *Mother Jones*, January/February 2003, http://www.motherjones.com/news/feature/2003/01/ma_207_01.html (accessed June 15, 2008).

7. Erika Engelhaupt, "Do Food Miles Matter?" *Environmental Science and Technology*, April 16, 2008, http://pubs.acs.org/subscribe/journals/esthag-w/2008/apr/science/ee_foodmiles.html (accessed June 15, 2008).

8. Kim Severson, "Local Carrots with a Side of Red Tape," *New York Times*, October 17, 2007, http://www.nytimes.com/2007/10/17/dining/17carr.html (accessed June 15, 2008).

9. Langston, "Many Barriers Keep Fresh, Organic Food Out of School Lunches."

10. Vanessa Zajfen, *Fresh Food Distribution Models for the Greater Los Angeles Region: Barriers and Opportunities to Facilitate and Scale Up Distribution of Fresh Fruits and Vegetables*, Center for Food & Justice, (Los Angeles, CA: Occidental College, March 2008), 9.

11. Barbara Kingsolver, Steven L. Hopp, and Camille Kingsolver, *Animal, Vegetable, Miracle: A Year of Food Life*, (New York: HarperCollins, 2007), 134-135.

12. Lauren Duffy, "The Story of a Meal," *Edible San Diego*, Summer 2008, 27-29.

13. Aley Kent, Heifer International, phone interview, June 12, 2008.

14. Jim Hayes, phone interview, June 15, 2008.

15. House Committee on Agriculture, Subcommittee on Livestock, Dairy, and Poultry, *Hearing on Review of Animal Identification Systems*, 110th Cong., 2nd sess., March 11, 2008.

16. U.S. Department of Agriculture, "National Animal Identification System (NAIS)", April 29, 2009, http://animalid.aphis.usda.gov/nais/index.shtml

17. Ibid.

18. Shannon Hayes, "Tag, We're It," *New York Times*, March 10, 2009, http://www.nytimes.com/2009/03/11/opinion/11hayes.html?th&emc=th (accessed March 26, 2009).

19. Karlene Lukovitz, "Marketing to Kids: FTC, CBBB Weigh In

With Reports," *Marketing Daily*, July 30, 2008, http://www.mediapost.com/publications/?fa=Articles.showArticleHomePage&art_aid=87528

20. Ibid.

21. Pete Hardin, "IGF-1 in rbGH-Milk Linked to Increased Human 'Twinning,'" *The Milkweed*, Issue No. 323, June 2006; http://www.centerforfoodsafety.org/rbGH2.cfm

22. U.S. Department of Agriculture, *Dairy 2007, Part 1: Reference of Dairy Cattle Health and Management Practices in the United States*, (USDAAPHI-VS, Centers for Epidemiology and Animal Health: Fort Collins, CO) 2007, 79.

23. FrameWorks Institute, "Perceptions of the U.S. Food System: What and How Americans Think About Their Food," W.K. Kellogg Foundation, 2005.

24. U.S. Department of Agriculture, WIC Fact Sheet, "The Special Supplemental Nutrition Program for Women, Infants and Children", April 2009, http://www.fns.usda.gov/wic/WIC-Fact-Sheet.pdf

25. U.S. Department of Agriculture, "Special Supplemental Nutrition Program for Women, Infants and Children: Revisions in the WIC Food Packages; Interim Rule," December 6, 2007; http://www.fns.usda.gov/wic/regspublished/wicfoodpkginterimruletxt.txt

26. U.S. Department of Agriculture, WIC Farmers Market Nutrition Program Fact Sheet, August 2008, http://www.fns.usda.gov/wic/WIC-FMNP-Fact-Sheet.pdf

27. U.S. Department of Agriculture, "Special Supplemental Nutrition Program for Women, Infants and Children: Revisions in the WIC Food Packages; Interim Rule," December 6, 2007.

28. Alan Beattie, "US farm bill unlikely to aid good nutrition," *Financial Times*, October 17, 2007, http://www.ft.com/cms/s/0/9459cdec-7cde-11dc-aee2-0000779fd2ac.html?nclick_check=1 (accessed August 2, 2008).

29. Food Democracy Now!, http://www.fooddemocracynow.org/

30. Craig Minowa and Ronnie Cummins, "Junk Food Potato Chips and Chocolate Now Being Fed to Cattle, *Organic Bytes #142,* Organic Consumers Association, August 21, 2008, http://www.organicconsumers.org/bytes/ob142.cfm.

7. LABELING

1. FrameWorks Institute, "Perceptions of the U.S. Food System: What and How Americans Think About Their Food," 9-10.

2. Edith Honan, "New York chain eateries must post calorie counts,"

Reuters, January 22, 2008, http://www.reuters.com/article/topNews/idUSN2255156520080123

3. Arthur Gregg Sulzberger, "Multnomah County board backs labeling on menus," *The Oregonian*, August 1, 2008, http://www.oregonlive.com/news/oregonian/index.ssf?/base/news/121756290747020.xml&coll=7; Peter Korn, "Menu-label law may be hard to swallow," *The Portland Tribune*, November 6, 2008, http://www.portlandtribune.com/news/story.php?story_id=122592640737182900

4. Emily Keller, "Menu labeling will take effect soon," *Sammamish Review*, August 13, 2008, http://sammamishreview.com/2008/08/13/menu-labeling-will-take-effect-soon (accessed August 24, 2008).

5. Patrick McGreevy, "New law will require California chain restaurants to display calorie counts," *Los Angeles Times*, September 30, 2008, http://articles.latimes.com/2008/sep/30/local/me-arnold30

6. Sarah E. White, "Philadelphia passes strictest menu labeling law," CalorieLab, November 10, 2008, http://calorielab.com/news/2008/11/10/philadelphia-passes-strictest-menu-labeling-law/

7. Michele Simon, *Appetite for Profit: How the Food Industry Undermines Our Health and How to Fight Back*, (New York, NY: Nation Books, 2006), 200–205.

8. Harold Goldstein, "How We Eat and the Slow Food Nation," Commonwealth Club podcast, July 31, 2008, http://www.commonwealthclub.org/archive/08/08-07waters-audio.html (accessed August 23, 2008).

9. McDonald's USA, Nutrition Info, Bag A McMeal, http://nutrition.mcdonalds.com/nutritionexchange/bagMeal.do

10. Stephanie Saul, "Conflict on the Menu," *New York Times*, February 16, 2008, http://www.nytimes.com/2008/02/16/business/16obese.html?ex=1360818000&en=03a9b2ce9ce2979c&ei=5088&partner=rssnyt&emc=rss (accessed August 24, 2008).

11. Stephanie Saul, "Menu Fight Over Calories Leads Doctor to Reject Post,*New York Times*, March 4, 2008, http://www.nytimes.com/2008/03/04/business/04obese.html

12. Harold Goldstein, phone interview, September 3, 2008.

13. Associated Press, "Appeals court upholds calories-on-menus rule," February 17, 2009, http://www.crainsnewyork.com/article/20090217/FREE/902179985

14. U.S. Department of Agriculture Economic Research Service, "Adoption of Genetically Engineered Crops in the U.S.: Corn Varieties," July 2, 2008, http://www.ers.usda.gov/Data/BiotechCrops/ExtentofAdoptionT-

able1.htm

15. The Mellman Group, "Public Sentiment About Genetically Modified Food," Pew Initiative on Food and Biotechnology, March 2001, http://www.pewtrusts.org/uploadedFiles/wwwpewtrustsorg/Public_Opinion/Food_and_Biotechnology/2006summary.pdf

16. Associated Press, "Poll: Many Won't buy Genetically Modified Food," *CBS News*, May 11, 2008, http://cbs4.com/national/CBS.News.New.2.721469.html (accessed September 4, 2008).

17. Susan Q. Stranahan, "Monsanto Vs. The Milkman," *Mother Jones*, January/February 2004, http://www.motherjones.com/news/outfront/2004/01/12_401.html

18. Ibid.

19. Bruce Mohl, "Monsanto Intimidates Maine Dairy into Label Compromise," *Globe Newspaper Company*, December 25, 2003, http://www.purefood.org/monsanto/intimidate122903.cfm

20. Food and Water Watch, "Consumers Want Hormone-Free Milk Labels, New Poll Shows," April 5, 2007, http://www.foodandwaterwatch.org/press/releases/consumers-want-hormone-free-milk-labels-new-poll-article04032007

21. Kiki Hubbard, "rBGH-Free Labeling Fight Goes to Court," Envirovore.com, August 5, 2008, http://envirovore.com/content/view/209/9/

22. Agriculture Online, "Elanco acquires dairy supplement from Monsanto," August 20, 2008, http://www.agriculture.com/ag/story.jhtml?storyid=/templatedata/ag/story/data/1219248085580.xml

23. Marion Nestle, "Guess the sponsor: rbGH milk study," What to Eat Blog, July 22, 2008, http://whattoeatbook.com/2008/07/22/guess-the-sponsor-rbGH-milk-study/ (Accessed March 18, 2009).

24. Rick North, "Elanco Buys rBGH From Monsanto," August 21, 2008, Grassroots Netroots Alliance, http://www.grassrootsnetroots.org/articles/article_14256.cfm

25. Ibid, 1.

26. Rosalie Marion Bliss, "Added Dietary Sugars Are Now Easily Identified," U.S. Department of Agriculture Agriculture Research Service, February 27, 2006, http://www.ars.usda.gov/is/pr/2006/060227.htm

27. Center for Science in the Public Interest, "Where Added Sugar Comes From," http://www.cspinet.org/reports/sugar/sugarorigin.html

28. Michael Jacobson, "CSPI's Petition to the FDA to Require Better Sugar Labeling on Foods," Center for Science in the Public Interest, August 3, 1999, 3.

29. Department of Agriculture, "Mandatory Country of Origin Labeling of Beef, Pork, Lamb, Chicken, Goat Meat, Wild and Farm-raised Fish and Shellfish, etc.," *Federal Register* 74., no. 10, (January 15, 2009), http://www.regulations.gov/fdmspublic/component/main?main=DocumentDetail&o=0900006480821339

30. Michael Hansen, "Consumers Union's Comments on US Department of Agriculture (USDA) Agricultural Marketing Service (AMS) Interim Final Rule on Mandatory Country of Origin Labeling of Beef, Pork, Lamb, Chicken, Goat Meat, Perishable Agricultural Commodities, Peanuts, Pecans, Ginseng, and Macadamia Nuts AMS-LS-07-0081," Consumers Union, September 30, 2008, http://www.consumersunion.org/pub/core_food_safety/006204.html (accessed March 14, 2009).

31. Tom Vilsack, Letter to Industry, February 20, 2009, http://www.usda.gov/documents/0220_IndustryLetterCOOL.pdf (Accessed March 14, 2009).

32. Kalra, EK, "Nutraceutical - Definition and Introduction," *AAPS PharmSci* 5, no. 2 (2003), http://www.aapsj.org/view.asp?art=ps050325

33. Marion Nestle, *Food Politics: How the Food Industry Influences Politics and Health*, (Berkeley: University of California Press, 2002), 231.

34. Ibid., 240.

35. Marian Burros, "Health Claims Put FDA in a Corner," *New York Times*, February 19, 1986, http://www.nytimes.com/1986/02/19/garden/health-claims-on-food-put-fda-in-a-corner.html?sec=health

36. Nestle, *Food Politics*, 250.

37. Ibid., 257.

38. Ibid., 225.

39. Ibid., 229-230.

40. Ibid., 266.

41. Fred H. Degnan, "FDA's Recent Steps to Implement Pearson v. Shalal," *JANA Journal* 3, no 3. (Fall 2000), http://www.heart-disease-bypass-surgery.com/data/articles/74.htm

8. FOOD SAFETY

1. Brian Hughes, "Tomato Farmers Still Reeling From Salmonella Scare," Kansas City InfoZine, September 19, 2008, http://www.infozine.com/news/stories/op/storiesView/sid/30782/ (accessed September 23, 2008).

2. Charlotte Vallaeys, "USDA Considers Uniform Rules for Leafy Greens: "One-Size-Fits-All" Regulations Would Harm Sustainable Farm-

ers/Environment," The Cornucopia Institute, November 26, 2007.

3. Annys Shin and Ylan Q. Mui, "Whole Foods Recalls Beef Processed At Plant Long at Odds With USDA," *Washington Post,* August 10, 2008, http://www.washingtonpost.com/wp-dyn/content/article/2008/08/08/AR2008080802821.html

4. Marion Nestle, *Pet Food Politics: The Chihuahua in the Coal Mine,* (Berkeley: University of California Press, 2008), 117-119.

5. Stephen Langel, "House, Senate Due to Start Moving Food Safety Bills After Recess," *CongressNow,* April 3, 2009.

6. U.S. Food & Drug Administration, "Foodborne Pathogenic Microorganisms and Natural Toxins Handbook: Escherichia coli O157:H7," http://www.foodsafety.gov/~mow/chap15.html

7. Centers for Disease Control and Prevention, "Disease Listing: Escherichia coli General Information", March 27, 2008, http://www.cdc.gov/nczved/dfbmd/disease_listing/stec_gi.html#9

8. Eric Schlosser, *Fast Food Nation: The Dark Side of the All-American Meal,* (New York: Houghton Mifflin, 2001).

9. Jill Richardson, "Pet Food Politics: Why Our Pets Still Aren't Safe," Alternet, September 10, 2008, http://www.alternet.org/healthwellness/97989/pet_food_politics:_why_our_pets_still_aren%27t_safe/?page=2

10. Gary Onan, 2nd annual Wisconsin Local Food Summit, Eau Claire, WI, January 24, 2008.

11. Schlosser, *Fast Food Nation,* 203.

12. Ibid., 209.

13. U.S. Department Of Agriculture Food Safety And Inspection Service, FSIS Notice, "Changes In Sampling Frequency For E. Coli O157:H7 Testing In Raw Ground Beef," March 12, 2009 http://www.fsis.usda.gov/OPPDE/rdad/FSISNotices/18-09.pdf

14. Marion Nestle, *Safe Food: Bacteria, Biotechnology, and Bioterrorism,* (Berkeley: University of California Press, 2003), 47.

15. Health Care Without Harm, "Antibiotic Resistance and Agricultural Overuse of Antibiotics: What Health Care Food Systems Can Do," August 2002, www.noharm.org/details.cfm?ID=938&type=document.

16. Joint WHO/FAO/OIE Expert Workshop on Non-human Antimicrobial Usage and Antimicrobial Resistance, Geneva, December 1-3, 2003, Executive Summary, http://www.who.int/foodsafety/micro/meetings/nov2003/en/ (Accessed September 27, 2008).

17. AgriTalk: The Voice of Rural America, March 18, 2009, http://www.agritalk.com/podcast/p.php?file=2009-03-18_march_18-09.mp3

18. Sheldon Rampton and John Stauber, *Mad Cow USA: Could the Nightmare Happen Here?*, (Monroe, ME: Common Courage Press, 2002), 211.

19. Ibid.

20. "FDA Strengthens Safeguards for Consumers of Beef," FDA, April 23, 2008, http://www.fda.gov/bbs/topics/NEWS/2008/NEW01823.html (accessed September 26, 2008).

21. Consumers Union, "Consumers Union says FDA proposed restriction on animal feed leaves nation vulnerable to spread of Mad Cow Disease," October 4, 2005, http://www.consumersunion.org/pub/core_food_safety/002715.html (accessed September 26, 2008).

22. Consumers Union, "USDA needs to do more to ensure safety of American beef," http://www.consumersunion.org/pub/core_food_safety/002436.html

23. Charles Abbott, "Court bars meatpacker tests for mad cow," *Reuters*, August 29, 2008, http://www.reuters.com/article/domesticNews/idUSN2928450820080829 (Accessed September 26, 2008).

24. U.S. Department of Health and Human Services and U.S. Environmental Protection Agency, "Mercury Levels in Commercial Fish and Shellfish," February 2006, http://www.cfsan.fda.gov/~frf/sea-mehg.html (accessed September 27, 2008).

25. HealthyTuna.com, "Tuna Facts," http://www.healthytuna.com/about-tuna/tuna-facts

26. Stephanie Mencimer, "Why Mercury Tuna is Still Legal," *Mother Jones*, September/October 2008, http://www.motherjones.com/news/feature/2008/09/exit-strategy-tuna-surprise.html (accessed September 27, 2008).

27. U.S. Environmental Protection Agency, "Health Effects: Mercury," http://www.epa.gov/mercury/effects.htm (accessed September 27, 2008).

28. U.S. Environmental Protection Agency, "What You Need to Know about Mercury in Fish and Shelfish: 2004 EPA and FDA Advice," http://www.epa.gov/waterscience/fish/advice/ (accessed September 27, 2008).

29. Environmental Working Group, "Brain Food: Fish Women Should Avoid," http://www.ewg.org/safefishlist (accessed September 27, 2008).

30. Environmental Working Group, "Tuna Calculator," http://www.ewg.org/tunacalculator (accessed September 27, 2008).

31. Mencimer, "Why Mercury Tuna is Still Legal," *Mother Jones*.

32. Nestle, *Safe Food*, 55.

33. Ibid., 55-57.

34. Ibid.

35. Gardiner Harris, "Bipartisan Call for Food Safety Fixes," *New York Times*, March 11, 2009, http://www.nytimes.com/2009/03/12/health/policy/12fda.html?_r=3&partner=rss&emc=rss (Accessed March 14, 2009).

36. Collin Peterson, Agri-Talk radio program, March 18, 2009, http://www.agritalk.com/podcast/media/2009-03-18_march_18-09.mp3 (Accessed March 19, 2009).

9. PROTECTING CHILDREN

1. Nestle, *Food Politics*, Table 26, 208-209.

2. Marion Nestle,"Soft Drink "Pouring Rights": Marketing Empty Calories to Children, *Public Health Rep*. 115, no. 4 (Jul–Aug 2000): 309.

3. Ibid, 310.

4. Nestle, *Food Politics*, 206.

5. Frameworks Institute, "Perception of the U.S. Food System", 11.

6. U.S. Department of Agriculture, Food and Nuturition Service, "Foods of Minimal Nutritional Value," April 28, 2009, http://www.fns.usda.gov/cnd/menu/fmnv.htm

7. Nestle, *Food Politics*, 214.

8. Ibid., 213-214.

9. *Child Nutrition Promotion and School Lunch Protection Act of 2007*, S. 771, 110th Cong. 1st sess., http://www.govtrack.us/congress/bill.xpd?bill=s110-771

10. Senate Committee on Agriculture, Nutrition, and Forestry, *Beyond Federal School Meal Programs: Reforming Nutrition for Kids in Schools*, 110th Cong., 2nd sess., March 31, 2009.

11. Senate Committee on Agriculture, Nutrition, and Forestry, *Testimony of Connie K. Boldt, School Food Director, Knoxville Community School District on Improving Nutrition For America's Children in Difficult Economic Times*, 110th Cong., 2nd sess., March 4, 2009.

12. U.S. Department of Agriculture, Food and Nutrition Service, "Healthier US School Challenge: Recognizing Nutrition ·Excellence in Schools," http://www.fns.usda.gov/tn/healthierus/index.html

13. Senate Committee on Agriculture, Nutrition, and Forestry, *Testimony of Connie K. Boldt, School Food Director, Knoxville Community School District on Improving Nutrition For America's Children in Difficult Economic Times*.

14. USDA Food and Nutrition Service, "Fresh Fruit and Vegetable

Program,"http://www.fns.usda.gov/cnd/FFVP/FFVPHistory.htm (accessed September 27, 2008).

15. Associated Press, "Children Targets of $1.6 Billion in Food Ads," *MSNBC*, July 29, 2008, http://www.msnbc.msn.com/id/25914206/ (accessed September 27, 2008).

16. Ibid.

17. Campaign for a Commercial Free Childhood, http://www.commercialfreechildhood.org/issues/overview.html (Accessed September 27, 2008).

18. *An Act Relative to the Public Health Impact of Commercialism in Schools*, Massachusetts H.B. 489, " May 2007, http://www.mass.gov/legis/bills/house/185/ht00/ht00489.htm (accessed September 27, 2008).

19. Multinational Monitor, "Commercializing Childhood: The Corporate Takeover of Kids' Lives: An interview with Susan Linn," July/August 2008, http://www.multinationalmonitor.org/mm2008/072008/interview-linn.html

20. Michele Simon, *Appetite for Profit*, 263.

21. Michael Jacobson, "Petition to Ban the Use of Yellow 5 and Other Food Dyes, in the Interim to Require a Warning on Foods Containing These Dyes, to Correct the Information the Food and Drug Administration Gives to Consumers On the Impact of These Dyes on the Behavior of Some Children, and to Require Neurotoxicity Testing of New Food Additives and Food Colors," Center for Science in the Public Interest, June 3, 2008, 3.

22. "CSPI Urges FDA to Ban Artificial Food Dyes Linked to Behavior Problems," Center for Science in the Public Interest, June 2, 2008, http://www.cspinet.org/new/200806022.html (accessed October 1, 2008).

23. Ibid.

24. Ibid.

10. HUMAN AND ANIMAL RIGHTS

1. Sasha Khokha, "Teen Farmworker's Heat Death Sparks Outcry," *NPR*, June 6, 2008, http://www.npr.org/templates/story/story.php?storyId=91240378 (accessed October 31, 2008).

2. "Worker Died Pruning on Two Buck Chuck Co-Owner's Land," Decanter.com, June 13, 2008, http://www.decanter.com/news/258661.html (accessed October 31, 2008).

3. United Farm Workers, "Heat Regulation Summary," http://ufw.org/_page.php?menu=creating&inc=legislation/heatregs/summary.html

4. Jason Lefkowitz, "The Short Life and Preventable Death of Maria Isabel Vasquez Jimenez," CtWconnect, June 2, 2008, http://www.changetowin.org/connect/2008/06/the_short_life_and_preventable.html (accessed October 31, 2008).

5. Jose Padilla, "A New, Fair Food System," Slow Food Nation, San Francisco, August 29, 2008.

6. Sasha Khokha, "Teen Farmworker's Heat Death Sparks Outcry," *NPR*, June 6, 2008, http://www.npr.org/templates/story/story.php?storyId=91240378 (accessed October 31, 2008).

7. Padilla, "A New, Fair Food System," Slow Food Nation.

8. Ibid.

9. Ibid.

10. Fred Grimm, "How About a Side Order of Human Rights," *The Miami Herald*, December 16, 2007, http://www.ciw-online.org/Fred_Grimm_Side_Order_Rigts.html (accessed October 28, 2008).

11. Ibid.

12. Amy Bennett Williams, "Five Plead Guilty in Immokalee Slavery Case," *Ft. Myers News-Press*, September 3, 2008, http://www.laborrights.org/creating-a-sweatfree-world/1679 (accessed October 28, 2008).

13. Coalition of Immokalee Workers, "About CIW," http://www.ciw-online.org/about.html (accessed October 28, 2008).

14. Andrew Clark, "Farmworkers Win Case Against McDonalds," *The Guardian*, April 11, 2007, http://www.guardian.co.uk/business/2007/apr/11/11 (accessed October 28, 2008).

15. Mica Rosenberg, "The Trouble with Tomatoes," *The Nation*, March 18, 2002, http://www.thenation.com/doc/20020401/rosenberg20020318 (accessed October 28, 2008).

16. Miriam Jordan, "Immigration Arrests Ex-Head of Meatpacking Plant," *Wall Street Journal*, October 31, 2008, http://online.wsj.com/article/SB122540155357885623.html?mod=googlenews_wsj (accessed October 31, 2008).

17. Associated Press, "Iowa Meatpacking Plant Raid Uncovers Illegal Immigrants, Underage Workers," *The Dallas Morning News*, July 29, 2008, http://www.dallasnews.com/sharedcontent/dws/news/nation/stories/072708dnnatchildlabor.6044762.html (accessed October 31, 2008).

18. Ibid.

19. Kerry Hall, Ames Alexander, and Franco Ordoñez, "The Cruelest Cuts: The Human Cost of Bringing Poultry To Your Table," *The Charlotte Observer*, September 30, 2008, http://www.charlotteobserver.com/595/

story/223415.html (accessed October 31, 2008).

20. Ibid.

21. Ibid.

22. Ames Alexander, Kerry Hall, Ted Mellnik, and Franco Ordoñez, "Workplace Inspections at 15-Year Low: OSHA Eases Poultry Companies' Penalties," *The Charlotte Observer*, October 1, 2008, http://www.charlotteobserver.com/595/story/223476.html (accessed November 1, 2008).

23. Ibid.

24. Ibid.

25. Jennifer Dillard, "A Slaughterhouse Nightmare: Psychological Harm Suffered by Slaughterhouse Employees and the Possibility of Redress through Legal Reform," *Georgetown Journal on Poverty Law & Violence* 15, no. 2, (Summer 2008): 1.

26. Ibid.," 7.

27. Ibid.," 6.

28. Humane Slaughter Act, http://www.animallaw.info/statutes/stusfd7usca1901.htm (accessed November 2, 2008).

29. Dr. Temple Grandin's Web Page, "Who is Dr. Temple, Grandin," http://www.grandin.com/temple.html (accessed November 2, 2008).

30. Joby Warrick, "They Die Piece by Piece: Investigation Reveals Rampant Cruelty in Industrial Slaughterhouses," *The Washington Post*, April 10, 2001, http://www.waitingforthestorm.com/en/slaughterhouse-washington (accessed November 3, 2008).

31. Ibid.

32. The Humane Farming Association, "HFA's Petition to Halt Slaughterhouse Crimes," http://www.hfa.org/hot_topic/usda_petition.html (accessed November 3, 2008).

33. Humane Society of the United States, "Undercover Investigation Reveals Rampant Animal Cruelty at California Slaughter Plant – A Major Beef Supplier to America's School Lunch Program," January 30, 2008, http://www.hsus.org/farm/news/ournews/undercover_investigation.html (accessed November 2, 2008).

34. Thomas.gov, "Downed Animal Protection Act of 1993," (accessed November 2, 2008).

35. Dillard, "A Slaughterhouse Nightmare," 6.

36. Thomas.gov, "Humane Methods of Poultry Slaughter Act of 1993," (accessed November 2, 2008).

37. Jesse McKinley, "A California Ballot Measure Offers Rights for Farm Animals," *International Herald Tribune*, October 24, 2008, http://

www.iht.com/articles/2008/10/24/america/24egg.php?page=1   (accessed November 2, 2008).

38. Ibid.

11. THE FARM BILL

1. Renee Johnson, "What Is the "Farm Bill"?, *Congressional Research Service*, Report for Congress, September 23, 2008, http://www.nationalaglawcenter.org/assets/crs/RS22131.pdf

2. Elanor Starmer and Timothy A. Wise, "Feeding at the Trough: Industrial Livestock Firms Saved $35 billion from Low Feed Prices," GDAE Policy Brief 07-03, (Medford, MA: Global Development and Environment Institute, Tufts University, December 2007), 2.

3. Cook, *Diet for a Dead Planet*, 132

4. Starmer and Wise, "Feeding at the Trough," 2.

5. Cook, *Diet for a Dead Planet*, 128.

6. Jim Hightower, *Eat Your Heart Out: How Food Profiteers Victimize the Consumer*, (New York: Random House, 1976), 39.

7. *Food, Conservation, and Energy Act of 2008*, H.R.2419, 110th Cong., 2nd sess., January 2008, http://frwebgate.access.gpo.gov/cgi-bin/getdoc.cgi?dbname=110_cong_bills&docid=f:h2419enr.txt.pdf

8. U.S. Department of Agriculture, Economic Research Service, "2008 Farm Bill Side-By-Side: Title I: Commodities," December 11, 2008, http://www.ers.usda.gov/farmbill/2008/titles/TitleIcommodities.htm

9. U.S. Department of Agriculture, Economic Research Service, "2008 Farm Bill Side-By-Side: Title Iv: Nutrition," August 20, 2008, http://www.ers.usda.gov/FarmBill/2008/Titles/TitleIVNutrition.htm, (accessed October 11, 2008).

10. Hank Herrera, email to author, October 9, 2008.

11. U.S. Department of Agriculture, Economic Research Service, "2008 Farm Bill Side-By-Side: Title Iv: Nutrition," August 20, 2008, http://www.ers.usda.gov/FarmBill/2008/Titles/TitleIVNutrition.htm (accessed October 11, 2008).

12. U.S. Department of Agriculture Food and Nutrition Service, "Supplemental Nutrition Assistance Program," http://www.fns.usda.gov/fsp/applicant_recipients/eligibility.htm#income (accessed October 13, 2008).

13. Andrea Carlson, Mark Lino, WenYen Juan, Kenneth Hansno, P. Peter Basiotis, "Thrifty Food Plan, 2006," USDA Center for Nutrition Policy and Promotion, April 2007, 7.

14. USDA Center for Nutrition Policy and Promotion, "Official USDA

Food Plans: Cost of Food at Home at Four Levels, U.S. Average, August 2008," September 2008.

15. Carlson, Lino, Juan, Hansno, Basiotis, "Thrifty Food Plan, 2006," 9.

16. Julie Thayer, Carolyn Murphy, John Cook, Stephanie Ettinger de Cuba, Rosa DaCosta, and Mariana Chilton, "The Real Cost of a Healthy Diet," C-SNAP at Boston Medical Center and The Philadelphia Grow Project at Drexel Univesrity, September 2008, 4.

17. Ibid.

18. Jane Black, "A Fresh Break For the Needy: Market Vouchers Aid Families on Assistance," *Washington Post*, May 27, 2009.

19. Thayer, Murphy, Cook, Ettinger de Cuba, DaCosta, and Chilton, "The Real Cost of a Healthy Diet," 5.

20. Rodale Institute, October 5, 2008.

21. Tim LaSalle and Paul Hepperly, "Regenerative Organic Farming: A Solution to Global Warming," Rodale Institute, July 5, 2008, 5.

22. Ibid., 1.

23. Ibid.,1.

24. Ibid., 3.

25. USDA Natural Resources Conservation Service, "Conservation Security Program," September 19, 2008, http://www.nrcs.usda.gov/programs/csp/ (accessed October 11, 2008).

26. Michael Pollan, "Power Steer," *New York Times Magazine*, March 31, 2002, http://www.michaelpollan.com/article.php?id=14 (accessed October 13, 2008).

27. Senate Committee on the Judiciary, Sub-Committee on Antitrust, Competition Policy and Consumer Rights, *Written testimony of the Organization for Competitive Markets*, 110th Cong., 2nd sess., May 7, 2008, http://www.competitivemarkets.com/index.php?option=com_content&task=view&id=110 (accessed October 13, 2008).

28. Ibid.

29. Ibid.

30. Tom Philpott, "If deals go through, three firms will own 90 percent of the U.S. beef market," Gristmill, March 5, 2008, http://gristmill.grist.org/story/2008/3/5/13322/15057

31. Mary Hendrickson and William Heffernan, "Concentration of Agricultural Markets," University of Missouri Department of Rural Sociology, April 2007.

32. Ibid.

33. Tom Philpott, "Meat Wagon: Beef Behemoth," Gristmill, March 5,

2008, http://gristmill.grist.org/story/2008/3/5/13322/15057

34. Ibid.

35. Mark Dowie, "Meat Packing Industry's Forward Contracting Captive Supplies Personifies 'Monopoly Capitalism,'" *Range Magazine*, January 2003, http://www.mindfully.org/Food/2003/Meat-Packing-Monopoly-Capitalism23jan03.htm

CONCLUSION

1. "Ronnie Cummins, "Organic Bytes #142," Organic Consumers Association, August 21, 2008, http://organicconsumers.org/forum/index.php?s=45fb4350411bb05e8d2a1d876116e4d1&showtopic=1957 (accessed October 21, 2008).